LEGENDS OF WARFARE

AVIATION

C-47 Skytrain

The "Gooney Bird" from Douglas

DAVID DOYLE

SCHIFFER MILITARY

4880 Lower Valley Road   Atglen, PA 19310

Designed by Christopher Bower
Cover design by Christopher Bower
Front cover image courtesy of Rich Kolasa
Type set in Impact/Minion Pro/Univers LT Std

ISBN: 978-0-7643-6790-8
Printed in India

Published by Schiffer Publishing, Ltd.
4880 Lower Valley Road
Atglen, PA 19310
Phone: (610) 593-1777; Fax: (610) 593-2002
Email: Info@schifferbooks.com
Web: www.schifferbooks.com

For our complete selection of fine books on this and related subjects, please visit our website at www.schifferbooks.com. You may also write for a free catalog.

Schiffer Publishing's titles are available at special discounts for bulk purchases for sales promotions or premiums. Special editions, including personalized covers, corporate imprints, and excerpts, can be created in large quantities for special needs. For more information, contact the publisher.

We are always looking for people to write books on new and related subjects. If you have an idea for a book, please contact us at proposals@schifferbooks.com.

Acknowledgments

This book would not have been possible without the generous assistance and resources of many friends and institutions, among them Tom Kailbourn, Rich Kolasa, Scott Taylor, Dana Bell, the National Museum of the United States Air Force, the Air Force Material Command History & Heritage Directorate, the San Diego Air and Space Museum, and the National Archives. All photos not otherwise credited are from the collection of the National Museum of the United States Air Force. Many of the photos in this book were scanned by my wife, Denise, without whose help, encouragement, and support this book would not have been possible.

Contents

Introduction

There are few aircraft in the world as iconic as the C-47 and its civil cousin, the DC-3. Even today, over seventy years into its history, the silhouette of a C-47 is used when illustrating any airborne operation. These aircraft soldiered on in their military form well beyond the usual lifetime of a military aircraft and, in fact, evolved into a combat aircraft long after most of its contemporaries had been relegated to the scrap heap. Surplus C-47s formed the backbone of the post–World War II commercial aviation industry, not only in the United States but also abroad.

The evolution of the aircraft that became the Douglas C-47 began in 1932, when the potential of the Boeing Model 247 became known—a year before it would actually fly. The all-metal, twin-engine model 247 would be easier to maintain, more comfortable and faster than the aircraft that then dominated the US airline industry, and able to fly cross-country in twenty hours, with stops along the way—seven hours faster than competitors. United Air Lines ordered sixty examples of the revolutionary aircraft, a breathtakingly large order for the time. This order tied up Boeing production for some time. Other airlines, including notably Transcontinental & Western Air (T&WA), wanted the aircraft but were told that no aircraft could be delivered to them until the United order had been completely filled. Not lost on T&WA vice president of operations (and later president of TWA, as T&WA became known), Jack Frye, was the fact that both Boeing and United Air Lines were owned by United Aircraft and Transport Corporation.

Accordingly, on September 20, 1932, an agreement was signed between T&WA and Douglas Aircraft to develop a competitive twin-engine airliner, the Douglas Commercial type 1 (DC-1). Following tests, TWA bought the DC-1 and, more importantly, ordered twenty improved models, which were designated DC-2.

The DC-2, of which 160 examples were sold to various civil airlines, was 2 feet longer than the DC-1. This change increased the passenger capacity to fourteen. While the Army Air Corps had done some testing of the DC-1, the government opted to wait for the successor before placing orders; however, it was the Navy that was the first branch to actually place an order for the DC-2, with five examples being ordered: three for the Navy itself and two for the Marine Corps. The aircraft were designated R2D-1 and were used for staff transport.

The War Department finally bought an aircraft, which was designated XC-32 and, following testing, was assigned to Bolling Field outside Washington, DC, for use as a VIP transport.

The XC-32 was followed by an order for eighteen C-33 transports, the first aircraft based on Douglas Commercial types to be specifically adapted for service as a military cargo aircraft. The C-33 lacked the seats and other comfort amenities of the DC-2 but had a reinforced floor. On the port side of the aft fuselage, a large cargo door was installed. While the C-33 was devoid of virtually all comfort features, that was not the case for all Army Air Corps aircraft based on the DC-2. Two YC-34 aircraft were purchased as well. These fourteen-seat aircraft were appointed similarly to a stock DC-2 and were used as transport for the secretary of war and were assigned to the 1st Staff Squadron at Bolling Field.

The Air Corps purchased a smattering of other aircraft types based on the DC-2 before shifting their focus to a transport based on the larger DC-3. The other DC-2-based aircraft, the C-38, C-39, C-41, and C-42, were produced in modest quantities and are illustrated in the following pages. In addition, when the US became involved in World War II, twenty-four civil DC-2s were impressed into military service and assigned the designation C-32A.

When it was introduced in 1933, the Douglas DC-1 prototype provided the template for the DC-2, DC-3, and C-47 families of transport aircraft, which would revolutionize commercial air travel and dependably serve the civil airlines and the military for decades to come. In a photo of the DC-1 prototype, on the rudder are Department of Commerce license number X-223Y and T&WA's plane number, 300.

The DC-1 was Douglas Aircraft's response to an August 1932 requirement issued by T&WA (Transcontinental & Western Airlines) for a new passenger aircraft of all-metal construction, capable of taking off, fully loaded, after the loss of one of the engines. Despite T&WA's requirement that the aircraft be a trimotor design, Douglas proposed the DC-1 as a twin-engine aircraft. The one-off prototype is shown at Clover Airfield, at Douglas's Santa Monica, California, plant, sometime between its rollout on June 23, 1933, and its first flight, on July 1.

The main cabin of the DC-1 had seats for twelve passengers, with an aisle between the seats. The cabin was tall enough to allow occupants to stand upright in the aisle. Racks for personal items were above the seats.

The DC-1 underwent an intensive series of test flights in 1933. In July of that year, the airplane landed at Wright Field, Ohio, as seen here, where personnel from the Army Air Development Center evaluated and test-flew the plane.

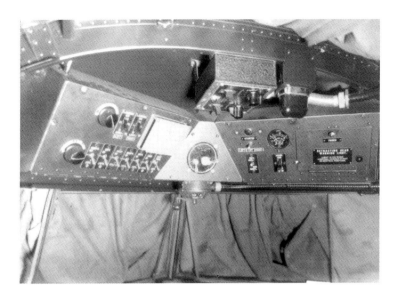

As seen from the pilot's position in the left side of the cockpit of the DC-1, a control panel was above the windshield, which has a canvas cover over it. On the left side are electrical switches for various systems. At the center is the ignition selector. On the right are the starter switch, amp meter, and fuse box.

The pilot's (*left*) and copilot's control wheels were mounted on yokes. Rudder pedals were below the main instrument panel. A floor-mounted console held the throttles and the controls for the propellers and fuel mixture.

Following the successful testing of the DC-1, Douglas Aircraft unveiled an improved version, the DC-2, in 1934. The DC-2, which went into series production, was 2 feet longer than the DC-1 and could seat fourteen passengers. Other improvements included brakes for the main landing gear, wing flaps, stressed-skin construction, and a redesigned rudder. A prominent difference from the DC-1 was the pair of landing lights jutting from the nose of the DC-2. A door with a curved top was to the lower rear of the cockpit. *San Diego Air and Space Museum*

On September 30, 1936, the Army Air Corps took delivery of one DC-2, serial number 36-1 and manufacturer's number 1414, installing military instruments and radio equipment and redesignating the aircraft the XC-32. In addition to Air Corps markings, the aircraft was distinguished by a radio direction-finder loop antenna and two radio masts atop the fuselage.

On its left side, the XC-32 had a door to the lower rear of the cockpit, a door for passengers aft of the wing, and what appears to be an access door between the passengers' door and the horizontal stabilizer. As was the case with the DC-2, the pitot tube was on the bottom of a mast below the nose.

Between May 1936 and January 1937, the Army Air Corps accepted eighteen C-33s, similar in general design to the XC-32 but built specifically as a military transport. A data stencil below the cockpit side windows reads, "WRIGHT FIELD / U.S. Army C-33 / A.C. 36-70." That serial number, 36-70, identifies this as the first C-33, which was delivered to the Army on May 22, 1936. The engines for the C-33s were the Wright Cyclone R-1820-25.

A C-33 is resting on a tarmac at March Field, California, on November 11, 1936, with an Aeronca C-2 airplane parked next to it. The C-33 featured a reinforced main-cabin floor, a large cargo door on the left side, and a detachable cargo boom that could be installed on the fuselage above the cargo door.

The third C-33, serial number 36-72, is painted in Olive Drab over Neutral Gray camouflage. A "football" radio direction-finder antenna is on the fuselage top, aft of the cockpit canopy and between two radio antenna masts.

A worker is operating a chain hoist on a tripod boom attached to fittings on the upper fuselage of a C-33. The cargo door was 5 feet high and consisted of two panels, which could be locked together and opened as a single door or could be operated as separate doors. When operated as a single door, the unit swung forward when opened.

In 1937, the US Army procured two YC-34s, which were service-test versions of the XC-32, assigning them serial numbers 36-345 and 36-346. They were used as VIP transports. The first one was relegated to an instructional airframe after being damaged in a landing accident, and the second one was destroyed in a crash in December 1942.

One of the two Douglas YC-34s is parked at an airfield during service as a transport for the secretary of war. The plane had a natural-metal finish and red, white, and blue stripes on the rudder, and the round insignia of Bolling Field, in Washington, DC, and the flag of the secretary of war are on the side of the aft fuselage. *San Diego Air and Space Museum*

The Douglas C-39, of which the US Army accepted thirty-five units in 1939, combined the basic fuselage and outer wing panels with the center-wing and engine-nacelles assembly, landing gear, and tail assembly of the Douglas DC-3. This entailed a larger dorsal fin and a rudder with a broader chord and entirely different shape than that of the C-33. This example had a fillet at the bottom of the dorsal fin.

A heavy-duty tractor is towing a C-39. A close inspection of the data stencil below the side window of the cockpit reveals that this aircraft was assigned serial number 30-499, which corresponds to the first C-39. On the C-39s, the two protruding landing lights on the nose were eliminated, and a landing light was installed in the leading edge of each wing.

In a left-rear view of a C-39, a small, rectangular window is located between the cargo door and the rear passenger's window. The second passenger's window is on an emergency exit panel, the lines of which are faintly visible.

This C-39 was photographed at the San Antonio Air Depot, in Texas, in 1940. A direction-finder loop antenna is on the top of the fuselage to the rear of the cockpit. The curved lens for the left landing light is faintly visible on the leading edge of the wing, toward the engine nacelle. A small, round window is toward the rear of the cargo door, and a similar window is on the fuselage aft of the door.

CHAPTER 1
C-47 and C-53

While the DC-2 was a success, American Airlines wanted something bigger, and with a twist. American wanted something akin to a flying Pullman sleeper car, with the seating area capable of being converted to a sleeping area. Following an appeal by American Airlines president C. R. Smith to Donald Douglas for such an aircraft—an appeal backed up with a promise of a twenty-aircraft order—Douglas tasked chief engineer Arthur A. Raymond to develop such an aircraft, to be dubbed the Douglas Sleeper Transport (DST). The fuselage of the new aircraft was more rounded and, as a result, 26 inches wider than that of the DC-2, as well as being 2½ feet longer. The DST, which could seat twenty-eight people or sleep fourteen, made its first flight on December 17, 1935.

Not all airlines were interested in having overnight sleeper aircraft, so Douglas modified the design to create an all-seat aircraft intended for daytime routes. Seating twenty-eight passengers, this version of the DST was designated the DC-3.

The aircraft were offered with the buyer's choice of either the nine-cylinder Wright SGR-1820 Cyclone 9 for the DC-3 or the fourteen-cylinder Pratt & Whitney SIC-S (R-1830) Twin Wasp, in what was designated the DC-3A. A second Cyclone-powered variant was offered, the DC-3B, which had half convertible seats (like the DST) and half standard airliner seating.

The DC-3 was immediately popular with the airline industry and also attracted the attention of the military. The first military version of the DC-3 was the one-off C-41A, which was delivered in September 1939. This aircraft, based on the DC-3A and powered by the R-1830-21, featured swivel seating in the passenger cabin and was naturally equipped with military radios and instruments. Like many of its Douglas transport predecessors, it was assigned to the 1st Staff Squadron, Bolling Field, for use as staff and VIP transport.

The next DC-3-type aircraft delivered for military use were C-53 Skytrooper aircraft. The C-53 was more closely akin to the DC-3 than its more famous sibling, the C-47. The C-53 lacked the reinforced metal floor of the C-47, instead retaining the hollow-core plywood floor of the DC-3, and, more noticeable to observers, the C-53 also lacked the large cargo doors of the C-47. Instead, the aircraft was equipped with an airline-type passenger door. The ninety-two-unit C-53 contract, number W-535-AC-18393, was announced on June 26, 1941.

The full aircraft model number was C-53-DO, with the DO indicating that the aircraft were built at the Douglas Santa Monica facility. At the time the contract was awarded, Douglas was building DC-3s in the Santa Monica plant, and adding the C-53s to that production line was the logical thing to do. The first of the aircraft to be completed was C-53-DO USAAF serial number 41-20045, which was delivered to the USAAF on October 15, 1941. Following the Japanese attack on Pearl Harbor, the DC-3s alongside the C-53s on the assembly line were impressed into military service, becoming C-48, C-49, and C-50 models—the different designations being the result of different specifications the aircraft had been built to, which had been assigned by their initial buyers: American Airlines, Pennsylvania Central, TWA, Eastern Airlines, Delta, United, etc.

However, even prior to the award of the contract for C-53 production, in July 1940 the military had reached an informal agreement with Douglas to produce two new DC-3 variants, the C-47 and the Navy R4D. The R4D-1 differed from the C-47 in having Navy-specified radios and instruments. Forty of the Army-contracted aircraft were produced for the Navy as well and were also R4D-1 types.

That agreement was formalized on September 16, 1940, when Douglas was awarded contract W535-AC-15847. This contract called for the production of 186 C-47s and thirteen R4D-1 aircraft, plus spare parts. Delivery of the aircraft was specified to begin with two in May 1941 and to be concluded with twenty in November of that year.

Change order #1 subsequently added an additional 363 C-47s and a further fourteen R4D-1s, for a total of 579 aircraft, with production continuing until April 1942.

Change order #2, issued in January 1941, reduced the number of C-47s to 575. This change was made in order to allow for the production of four C-48/C-48A Personnel Transports.

Because the Santa Monica plant was bustling with not only the above aircraft, but also DB-7 and A-20 bombers, production of the C-47, dubbed the Skytrain, would take place in a new, purpose-built military aircraft plant to be constructed by Douglas and then sold to the government over a five-year period. Situated in Long Beach, California, the newly built plant had no windows, had blackout doors, and had underground bomb shelters for the estimated 18,000 people who would work there.

Ground was formally broken for the Long Beach plant on November 22, 1940, and the plant was officially dedicated on Friday, October 17, 1941. Production of aircraft parts and assemblies at the facility began several months before the buildings were complete.

The aircraft would be built on a cost-plus-fixed-fee basis, which was initially set at 6 percent. As future contracts were issued, this fee was reduced to 4 percent. The first C-47 was completed in February 1941, and the second in April. It would be January 1942 before the third example was completed and the plant was in full production. The first aircraft, C-47-DL 41-7722—the "DL" identifier

The Douglas DC-3 provided the template for the C-47. The direct predecessor of the DC-3 was called the Douglas Skysleeper Transport (DST), depicted here. It featured four passenger compartments with a total of fourteen upholstered seats, which could be folded in pairs to form seven berths, and seven more folding berths were mounted on the cabin ceiling. The DST had a second, higher row of small windows for the upper bunk beds, visible here. The Skysleeper could also be configured with twenty-eight seats for shorter-distance flights. American Airlines received the first Skysleeper in June 1936, and the first standard twenty-one-passenger DC-3 two months later. American ordered its early DST and DC-3 aircraft with passenger doors on the right side of the fuselage, as here. Later, left-side doors became standard both in civil and military aircraft. *San Diego Air and Space Museum*

denoting it was produced at the Douglas Long Beach plant—had its USAAF "689 Board," or engineering-evaluation inspection, in December 1941 and made its first flight on January 1, 1942.

The C-47-DL was akin to the DC-3A in that it was powered by a pair of Pratt & Whitney engines, specifically the R-1830-92 Twin Wasp. These engines, which had integral single-speed superchargers with an impeller gear ratio of 7.15 to 1, had a War Emergency horsepower rating of 1,200 hp each. Rather than the small passenger door of the DC-3 (or C-53), in the left side of the rear fuselage was a large three-section cargo door. Also, externally distinguishing the C-47 from the civil DC-3 was the Plexiglas astrodome for the navigator atop the forward fuselage.

Internally, the aircraft were bereft of all the niceties of the civil cousins, including a considerably simplified toilet. In other places in the floor were mounted tie-down rings for securing cargo, and, throughout, gone was the comfortable passenger seating; in its place were foldaway metal bench seats. The passenger windows had small plastic plugs in their centers to allow soldiers to defend the unarmed aircraft with their rifles if need be.

Beginning with the one hundredth C-47, which was accepted by the Army Air Force on April 16, 1942, the carpetless floor had patches of antiskid material put in place to help boot-clad paratroopers maintain their footing. Overhead, static lines were installed for release of paratrooper parachutes. Provisions for six external para-pack racks with both electrical and mechanical release were made. At aircraft 182, the cargo door was enlarged by 18 inches to accommodate jeeps, 37 mm and 75 mm guns, and other bulky cargo. The first aircraft so equipped was accepted on May 9, 1942.

Glider-towing provisions were added at aircraft 491, which was accepted on August 31, 1942.

The second C-47 contract, DA W-535-AC-167, was issued in June 1941. The two hundred aircraft on this contract, USAAF serial numbers 41-38564 through 41-38763, were intended for Defense Aid and were to be delivered between September and December 1942. Following the US entry into World War II, many of these aircraft were retained for use by the USAAF. Like in the previous contract, these aircraft were built in Long Beach.

In September 1941, contract W-535-AC-20669, the third for C-47-type aircraft, was awarded. These aircraft included seventy C-47-DLs, serial numbers 42-5635 through 42-5704, and fourteen R4D-1s. Most of these aircraft were turned over to the RAF, RAAF, or the Soviet Union, presumably to make up for the aircraft on contract -167, which the USAAF had diverted. However, serial numbers 42-5671 through 42-5704 were retained by the USAAF.

The final contract for C-47 production was DAW-535-AC-1043. A letter of intent for these 150 C-47s was signed on Christmas Eve 1941 and formalized on February 7, 1942. As indicated by the "DA" prefix in the contract number, these aircraft were intended for Defense Aid, specifically the RAF, China, and Russia, but once again, many of these were diverted to the USAAF.

Eight of the C-53 aircraft on contract W-535-AC-18393 of June 1941 were outfitted for Arctic operations, with extra fuel tanks, a C-47-style navigator's bubble, and winterization equipment. These eight aircraft were designated C-53B.

The June 1941 ninety-two-aircraft C-53 order was augmented by a contract for a further fifty examples in September. In January, forty additional C-53-DO aircraft were ordered for Defense Aid under contract AC-1040-DA, and the next month contract DAAC-1047 was issued for twenty-five more Defense Aid aircraft. Twelve more of the aircraft were delivered in June 1942, these aircraft having been preceded slightly by twenty DC-3s and DC-3As that were impressed into military service from civilian airlines and given the designation C-53C. Two DC-3s that had been ordered by Eastern Airlines were taken into military service by the Navy as R4D-2.

The Douglas C-41, of which only one was built, was the first aircraft based on the Douglas DC-3 that was purchased by the US government. Douglas built the C-41 in October 1938, and the US Army accepted it on the twenty-second of that month, assigning it serial number 38-502. Power was provided by powered by two Pratt & Whitney R-1830-21 900 hp engines. The plane was assigned as a VIP transport to the 1st Staff Squadron, at Bolling Army Airfield, Washington, DC. The C-41 survives, in the collection of the Mid America Flight Museum, Mount Pleasant, Texas. *San Diego Air and Space Museum*

The C-47-DL was the first full-production model of the Douglas DC-3 ("DL" stood for Douglas's Long Beach plant). Produced at Douglas Aircraft's Santa Monica and Long Beach, California, and Oklahoma City, Oklahoma, plants, the C-47 replaced the DC-3's passenger door with a large, split, cargo door. The engines were Pratt & Whitney R-1830-92 Twin Wasps, and the C-47 also had a wingspan that was 6 inches more than the DC-3's. The cockpit was equipped with Army-specified instruments, and the main cabin was spartan, lacking the plush upholstery of the civilian DC-3.

Douglas C-47-DL, serial number 41-7805, was one of the aircraft on the first C-47 contract, AC15847, issued by the US Army Air Forces. This C-47 was delivered on April 23, 1942, and was ferried to England later that year. It served at several air bases in that country until November 1942, when it transported members of the 503rd Parachute Infantry Battalion to Oran, Algeria, as part of Operation Torch. Following the war, this plane operated with Alitalia airlines and was destroyed by saboteurs in Ethiopia in 1975.

C-47-DL, serial number 41-18427, was delivered to the Army on July 5, 1942, and in World War II served successively with the Eighth Air Force and the 313th Transport Squadron, 31st Air Transport Group, Ninth Air Force. A number, "290," is painted on the nose. On the top of the fuselage aft of the cockpit are the astrodome and, to the left of it, an air scoop.

As seen in a left-front view of C-47-DL, 41-18427, a crew door with a curved top was present on the side of the forward fuselage, to the lower rear of the cockpit. The plane was camouflaged in Olive Drab over Neutral Gray. The left landing light is behind a curved lens on the leading edge of the wing. Aft of the engine cowlings, on the bottom of the engine nacelles, are the oil-cooler housings.

A frontal view of C-47-DL, serial number 41-18427, shows both landing lights, on each wing, as well as some details of the twin-strut main landing gears. *National Archives*

In an in-flight photo of C-47-DL, serial number 41-18427, the number "290" is visible on each side of the nose. The clear shell of the astrodome is missing, with a flat cover present over its opening.

The same C-47-DL, with "290" marked on the nose, is seen in flight from the lower forward-right quarter. The tail landing gear was non-retracting but could swivel 360 degrees, and during flight it was centered and locked. *National Archives*

The exhaust, incorporating a muff-type heat exchanger, is in view on the outboard side of the right engine nacelle of C-47-DL, 41-18427. Below the nose, and arranged close together, are the pitot-tube mast and a separate mast for a wire antenna.

Douglas C-47-DL, serial number 41-18427, is observed from above as it flies over the countryside. The cover over the fairing for the astrodome is clearly visible, to the left of the centerline of the top of the fuselage.

A final view of C-47-DL, 41-18427, shows the plane at an airfield, in a more weathered condition than in the preceding photos. The "290" number that was on the side of the nose has been sprayed over with paint, and a different marking (a partially erased "5"?) has been applied in that area.

The main cabin of the C-47, seen here facing forward, originally had inward-facing canvas troop seats, which folded up against the side walls when not in use. By the time this photo was taken, the canvas seats had been replaced by folding metal bench seats with safety belts. These were mounted on piano hinges and are shown folded down. *National Archives*

The metal troop seats are in their raised positions. On each side of the cabin, there were fourteen seats on three separate assemblies, two of which had five seat pans and one of which had four pans. Safety belts were attached to eyebolts on the sill running fore and aft behind the seats. Each passenger window had a small, removable plug, which troops could remove and fire small arms through.

The main compartment of the C-47 was equipped to transport litter patients, for medical evacuation operations. Here, three litters are installed, with the upper and center litters supported by brackets and braces, and the lower litter resting on the floor. The troop seats are folded down. To the far left is the cargo door.

	Specifications per USAAF Erection and Maintenance Manual												
Model	Engines	Takeoff hp	Propeller diameter	Cruising speed	Operating altitude	Integral fuel capacity (US gallons)	Range	Maximum payload	Wingspan	Length	Height (tailwheel on ground)	Wing area
C-47 Skytrain / R4D-1 / Dakota Mk. 1	Pratt & Whitney R-1820-92	1,200 each	11 ft., 7 in.	185	11,200 ft.	804	2,125 miles	9,450	95 ft., 0 in.	64 ft., 5.5 in.*	16 ft., 11.125 in.	884.2 ft.²
C-47A Skytrain / R4D-5 / Dakota Mk. III	Pratt & Whitney R-1820-92	1,200 each	11 ft., 7 in.	185	11,200 ft.	804	2,125 miles	9,450	95 ft., 0 in.	63 ft., 9 in.	16 ft., 11.125 in.	884.2 ft.²
C-47B Skytrain / R4D-6 / Dakota Mk. IV	Pratt & Whitney R-1820-92	1,200 each	11 ft., 7 in.	185	11,200 ft.	804	2,125 miles	9,450	95 ft., 0 in.	63 ft., 9 in.	16 ft., 11.125 in.	884.2 ft.²
C-53 Skytrooper / R4D-3 / Dakota Mk. II	Pratt & Whitney R-1820-90B	1,200 each	11 ft., 7 in.	185	11,200 ft.	804	2,125 miles	7,711	95 ft., 0 in.	64 ft., 5.5 in.	16 ft., 11.125 in.	884.2 ft.²

*63 ft., 9 in. with glider tow coupling

Aft of the main cabin was a lavatory, including a wash basin that was built into the corner of the compartment. *National Archives*

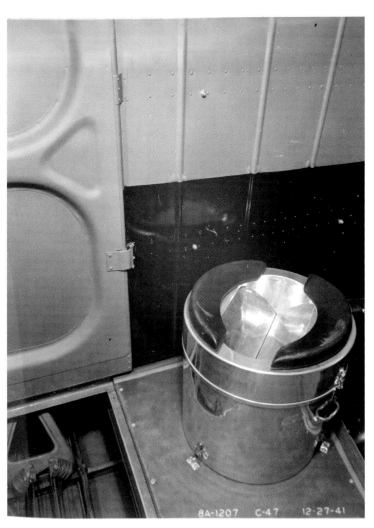

Also in the lavatory was a chemical toilet. *National Archives*

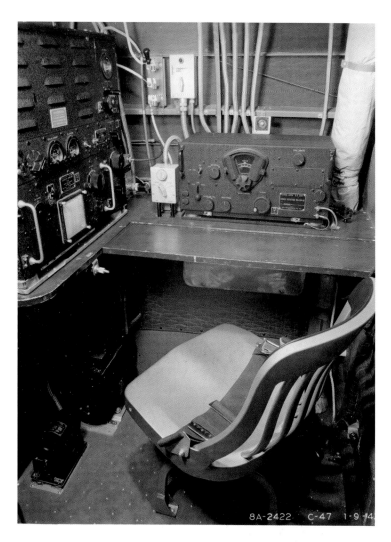

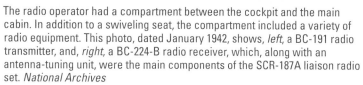

The radio operator had a compartment between the cockpit and the main cabin. In addition to a swiveling seat, the compartment included a variety of radio equipment. This photo, dated January 1942, shows, *left*, a BC-191 radio transmitter, and, *right*, a BC-224-B radio receiver, which, along with an antenna-tuning unit, were the main components of the SCR-187A liaison radio set. *National Archives*

As seen in a photo dated December 22, 1941, between the pilot's and copilot's seats was the control pedestal. On it were the throttle controls, carburetor mixture and air-temperature controls, propeller controls, rudder and aileron trim-tab controls, left and right engine fuel-selector controls, parking lock, and oil-cooler control levers. *National Archives*

Further details of the cockpit are displayed in another photo taken on December 21, 1941, including the control wheels and yokes, the rudder pedals, and the main instrument panel, which included separate instruments for the pilot, *left*, and the copilot, *right*. Atop the center of the instrument panel is a magnetic compass, directly below which is an azimuth indicator. *National Archives*

This is a view from the copilot's seat, looking toward the pilot's seat and the left side of the cockpit. The light-colored boxes on the side wall are, *left*, the pilot's radio receiver crystal filter, and, *right*, the pilot's interphone jack box. The dark-colored cylinder forward of these boxes is a fluorescent light. *National Archives*

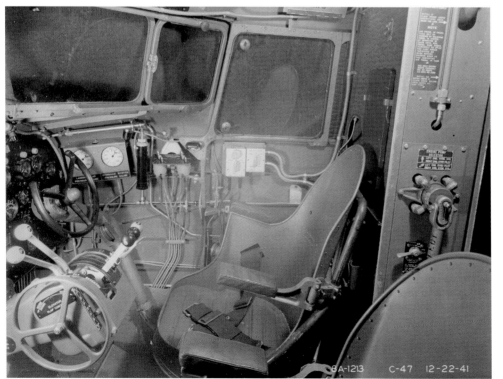

On the right wall of the cockpit are, *left to right*, pressure gauges for the landing-gear hydraulic system and the general hydraulic system, a fluorescent light, engine cowl-flap controls, and the copilot's interphone jack box and radio receiver crystal filter. To the far right are, *upper*, the hydraulic fluid sight gauge and hydraulic fluid filter neck, and, *lower*, the engine pump selector. To the right is the control pedestal. *National Archives*

Details of the copilot's seat (*foreground*) and the pilot's seat of the C-47 are in view. The copilot's seat cushion has been removed from the seat pan, but one is present on the pilot's seat. Both seats have upholstered backrests. Both seats have solid-metal outboard sides, with an armrest on top; the inboard sides of the seats have cutouts and pivoting arm rests, to enable the pilot and copilot to easily be seated or exit the seats. *National Archives*

A Pratt & Whitney R-1830-92 Twin Wasp radial engine for a C-47 is viewed from the right rear in a December 12, 1941, photo. On the rear of the engine are the accessories, and the engine mount is installed. Between the accessories and the engine cylinders is the inner ring assembly of the cowling. Around the cylinders is the exhaust collector ring. *National Archives*

A Pratt & Whitney R-1830-92 Twin Wasp engine installation in the right nacelle of a C-47 is the subject of this January 28, 1942, photograph. The upper inboard part of the engine support is visible to the upper left. Below the engine is the can-shaped oil cooler. *National Archives*

Three assembly-line workers, including two women, at Douglas Aircraft's plant in Long Beach, California, are preparing a section of the forward fuselage for riveting the aluminum-alloy skin to the frame. This section of fuselage was the upper part of what was designated as the flight compartment in C-47 maintenance instructions. Skin panels are pinned in place, and the man to the left is operating a riveting gun. The section of fuselage includes the upper part of the cockpit and the structure to the front of it. *Library of Congress*

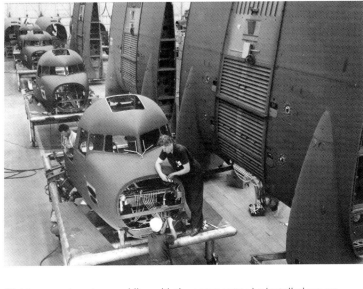

Flight-compartment assemblies with the noses yet to be installed are on trolleys alongside center-wing assemblies for Douglas C-47 transport planes at Douglas's Long Beach, California, plant. Openings for escape hatches are on the tops of the flight-compartment assemblies. The center-wing assemblies also include the engine nacelles. *Library of Congress*

On the assembly line at the Long Beach factory, to the left are center-wing assemblies, with flight-compartment assemblies (viewed from the rear) in the center and fuselage assemblies to the right. These components are moving toward the final assembly line, where they will be joined together to produce completed C-47s. *Library of Congress*

Partially assembled C-47s have reached the stage of assembly where their noses, flight compartments, fuselages, center-wing assemblies, engines, and main landing gear have been joined together. Outer-wing assemblies will soon be mounted on them. The upper half of the nose section of the C-47 was hinged, to form a door for accessing the rear of the main instrument panel. *Library of Congress*

On the Long Beach assembly line, partially constructed C-47s, possibly the same ones pictured in the preceding photograph, are awaiting the installation of their outer-wing assemblies. The nearest airframe is C-47-DL, serial number 41-18625 and manufacturer's serial number 4786, which would be delivered to the US Army Air Forces on October 26, 1942. *Library of Congress*

A row of C-47s, lacking their outer-wing assemblies, are under construction at the Long Beach plant. On the noses, three-digit numbers have been stenciled, next to which are placards with the same number preceded by the word "SHIP." These ship numbers represented the sequential number of the planes in C-47-DL production, starting with number 1, but were not the same as the manufacturer's serial numbers (manufacturer's serial numbers began at 4200). In the series of photos taken at the Long Beach plant, usually the ship numbers have been censored. Visible on the noses of the first three airframes are numbers 592, 593, and 594. *Library of Congress*

C-47-DL, serial number 41-18624 and manufacturer's serial number 4785, is awaiting installation of the outer-wing assemblies at the Long Beach plant. This aircraft would be delivered to the US Army on October 30, 1942. *Library of Congress*

The ship number on the side of the nose has been censored in this photo of a C-47-DL with its outer wings installed, at the Long Beach plant. On the bottom of the flight compartment, two objects are protruding downward. These are the aircraft's two 12-volt batteries, mounted on spring-loaded platform elevators, which facilitated lowering the batteries from the fuselage for maintenance or replacement. *Library of Congress*

In a final photo of C-47s under assembly at Douglas Aircraft's plant at Long Beach, California, in 1942, at the center is the airframe assigned serial number 41-18619. In the right and center background are more C-47 fuselages. In the foreground, workers' lunch boxes, hats, and jackets are on top of metal parts lockers. *Library of Congress*

The US Navy and the Marine Corps procured a version of the C-47, designated the R4D-1. Essentially, it was identical to the Army's C-47, with the substitution of USN-type instruments and radio equipment, and with Navy Bureau Numbers (BuNos) rather than Army serial numbers. Deliveries of the R4D-1s began in February 1942, starting with BuNo 3131. *National Archives*

The same R4D-1, numbered "81" on the nose, is viewed from the aft-left quarter. The national insignia is the style discontinued in May 1942, with a red circle in the center of the white star, on a blue background. Reportedly the stock camouflage of R4D-1s was Army-style Olive Drab over Neutral Gray. The rudder was decorated with horizontal red and white stripes and a vertical blue stripe. *National Archives*

LEFT SIDE VIEW

The Douglas R4D-1 numbered "81" presents its left-rear aspect to the camera. Power for these planes was provided by two Pratt & Whitney R-1830-92 engines. *National Archives*

A Navy R4D-1 flies over a populated area on November 2, 1942. The "3-R-3" code on the side of the cockpit stands for the third aircraft of Transport Squadron 3 (VR-3). *National Archives*

The 3-R-3 code of the same R4D-1, from VR-3, is faintly visible on the side of the cockpit in this second photo of the plane, on November 2, 1942. The version of the national insignia on the wings and the fuselage, a white star on a blue circle, remained in effect from May 1942 to June 1943. *National Archives*

A close examination of this photo of an R4D-1 in flight reveals that the 3-R-3 code is present on the forward fuselage. Also visible are the astrodome and the small, round plugs in the passengers' windows, for firing small arms through. *National Archives*

The designation C-49B-DO ("DO" stood for Douglas, Santa Monica) was given to three Eastern Airlines DC-3-201F passenger planes that the US Army Air Forces took possession of, after they had been modified to DC-3-387 standards. These planes were given USAAF serial numbers 41-7691 to 41-7693. All three C-49Bs were delivered to the Army in February 1942. This example sports bare-aluminum finish and red, white, and blue stripes on the rudder. *National Archives*

The interior of the main cabin of one of the three C-49B-DOs retained features of the civilian DC-3, including soundproofing, curtains for the windows, plush seats with armrests for the passengers, and baggage racks above the seats. *National Archives*

Shortly after the United States entered World War II, the US Army impressed this single Douglas DC-3, which had been ordered by Canadian Colonial Airways, immediately upon completion, designating it C-51. The engines were the Wright R-1820-83. The passenger door was on the right side of the fuselage. On the nose is the number "2." *National Archives*

Based on the DC-3, the Douglas C-53-DO was conceived as a dedicated troop transport. Instead of large cargo doors, it had a small door for passengers on the left side of the aft fuselage. The C-53s were equipped with twenty-eight individual metal bucket seats, arranged facing forward, and since the planes did not transport heavy cargo, the floor of the main cabin was not reinforced. The first C-53, serial number 41-20045, was delivered to the Army on October 15, 1941. This C-53 is marked "62" on the nose, and the photo was taken some time before December 11, 1941. *National Archives*

The same C-53-DO is observed from the front. The Hamilton Standard Hydromatic propeller blades had a metallic finish. *National Archives*

The C-53-DO numbered "62" was marked "62" over "10T" on the vertical fin. On the top of the left wing was marked "10T62." *National Archives*

On the C-53Ds, the twenty-eight individual troop seats of the earlier-model C-53s were replaced by twenty-eight hinged, metal seats attached to the sides of the main cabin, similar to those in the C-47. On the left side of the cabin, the forward module of five seat pans has been folded down. At the front of the cabin are two cabin fuel tanks. *National Archives*

The Mid America Flight Museum preserves in flightworthy condition a Douglas C-47-DL, serial number 42-32832, which was built in Santa Monica and delivered to the Army on February 11, 1943. This Skytrain had an illustrious operational career, transporting airborne troops to Sicily in Operation Husky in 1943, and dropping paratroopers and supplies and towing gliders in Italy, in Normandy on D-Day, and in Holland during Operation Market Garden. *Rich Kolasa*

The paint and markings of C-47-DL, 42-32832, replicate the Olive Drab over Neutral Gray camouflage, black and white invasion stripes, and squadron code of the plane around the time of D-day in Normandy in 1944. The "3A" code represents the 53rd Troop Carrier Squadron, part of the 61st Troop Carrier Group. The "M" on the tail was the aircraft's call letter. *Rich Kolasa*

CHAPTER 2
C-47A

At aircraft manufacturer's serial number 1032, the C-47 was replaced on the Douglas assembly line by the C-47A, which would become the most produced of all DC-3 variants, with a remarkable 5,253 being built at Long Beach and a new facility in Oklahoma. It was also at this time that the production block system was introduced. Production block assignment, which was used by many manufacturers on many types of aircraft, provided an easy way to track changes in aircraft that were not significant enough to cause an entirely new model suffix (A, B, etc.) to be assigned. The first C-47A built in Long Beach was thus a C-47A-1-DL.

The C-47A differed from the C-47 primarily in having a 24-volt electrical system rather than the 12-volt system of its predecessor. This was a result of a USAAF plan to standardize on 24-volt radio and electrical equipment.

Supplement number 2 to contract W-535-AC-20669 was signed on the last day of January 1942, calling for the production of 1,120 C-47A aircraft to carry the USAAF serial numbers 42-23300 through 42-24419 inclusive. The first C-47A-1-DL was completed on February 28, 1943, and accepted on March 4.

In April 1942, negotiations began for the procurement of an additional two thousand aircraft. These negotiations would go on until December 4, 1942, when at last contract W-535-AC-32725 was signed. The profit percentage on this contract was reduced to 4 percent, as opposed to the 5 percent or 6 percent of the prior contracts. Delivery of the aircraft under this contract was scheduled to begin in September 1943.

In July 1942, a further 134 C-47As were ordered by the Army on behalf of the Navy, who classified the aircraft as R4D-5. These aircraft were ordered on supplement 5 to contract W-535-AC-20669. Also, in July 1942 the final contract for C-53-type aircraft was issued, number 535-AC-26937. These 159 aircraft, designated C-53D, all of which were built in Santa Monica, began to be delivered in February 1943. Unlike the C-53 and C-53C aircraft, which had airliner-style seating, the C-53D had C-47-style seating. The C-53D also featured a 24-volt electrical system, like the C-47A.

At C-47A aircraft 1282, the type of cabin heater was changed. The original system, which was of a steam heat type, was replaced with a system that used the engine exhaust as a heat source. This change brought with it a complete redesign of the ducting, control valves, and distribution system.

Early on, with the order books at both Santa Monica and Long Beach swelling, not only with C-47 orders but also contracts for

A-20, A-26, SBD, and a host of other military aircraft, a new facility was needed. The Army had long been unhappy with the proximity of the two previously named plants to the coast, and the associated vulnerability. Further, labor demands in these areas were at a crisis state. Erecting a new plant, well inland, would relieve many pressures. This was consistent with War Department policy that had been established prior to US involvement in World War II.

On August 22, 1940, the Depression-era government-owned Reconstruction Finance Corporation created the Defense Plant Corporation. The new subsidiary was tasked with overseeing the construction of manufacturing facilities, which the government would then lease to defense contractors.

Influential members of the Oklahoma City, Oklahoma, community hoped to have either an air base or aircraft plant located in their city, and the Chamber of Commerce submitted a briefing paper to the War Department. The War Department responded with a request for a potential site for an aircraft maintenance facility—an air depot—and provided criteria for such a site. It should be on relatively flat ground, near existing railroads and paved roads, within 10 miles of Oklahoma City, and at least 4 miles from an oil field.

Local newspaperman W. P. "Bill" Atkinson, having seen the published criteria, bought such a property east of Oklahoma City and then traveled to Washington, DC, in hopes of selling the land to the government. On April 8, 1941, the War Department announced it would be building what was then termed the Midwest Air Depot on 960 acres in the area of Atkinson's property. Atkinson announced plans to construct a town nearby to house the expected influx of workers.

In January 1942, Douglas representatives inspected a 480-acre site east of the Midwest Air Depot and, finding it satisfactory, began planning to produce C-47s on the site.

Ground was officially broken for the government-owned, contractor-operated plant on July 4, 1942, although construction had actually begun on March 23. Thus, the "Oklahoma City" Douglas plant was actually in Midwest City. In October 1942, the Midwest Air Depot was renamed Tinker Field. Today the Douglas plant is Building 3001 of Tinker Air Force Base—and is still in Midwest City.

On March 11, 1943, the community of Midwest City was incorporated, encompassing the plant site. Contract W-535-AC-28405 was issued in August 1942 for two thousand C-47A aircraft to be built in the new plant.

Early in 1943, the plant began turning out C-47 parts, and in the first week of March 1943, just under a year after the building had been begun, the first complete Skytrain was rolled out, C-47A-DK serial number 42-92024. The DK code indicated that the aircraft was manufactured at the Oklahoma (Midwest) City plant.

The Douglas C-47A (including the USN and USMC version, the R4D-5) was the most numerous of the C-47 models, with over 5,250 units being completed at the plants in Long Beach and Oklahoma City. The C-47A replaced the 12-volt electrical system of the C-47 with a 24-volt system, and the C-47A had improved heating for the cabin. Shown here is C-47A-1-DK, serial number 42-92095, delivered on July 24, 1943. The "DK" suffix in the aircraft's nomenclature indicated that it was built at Douglas's Oklahoma City plant. *San Diego Air and Space Museum*

The cockpit of the C-47A was virtually identical to that of the C-47, with the pilot's seat, control yoke, and instruments on the left side, and the copilot's on the right. At the center was the control pedestal, with controls for the throttle, the carburetor mixture, propellers, trim tabs, fuel selection, and more. At the upper center, above the compass, is the altitude-limit switch.

Douglas C-47A-80-DL Skytrains are under assembly at the Long Beach, California, plant in early 1944. The second through fourth airframes are, respectively, serial numbers 43-15216, 43-15215, and 43-15215; the nearest plane is 43-15217. The four-digit numbers on the middles of the fuselages are not the manufacturer's numbers, but possibly the airframes' sequential numbers as C-47As. These C-47As were delivered to the Army between February 19 and 21, 1944. The banner in the center background reads, "WIN WITH WINGS."

Douglas C-47A-15-DK, serial number 42-92847, was delivered to the Army on March 6, 1944, and henceforth played an active role in World War II. Serving with the 87th Troop Carrier Squadron, the plane carried the squadron code "3X" and the call letter "W" and operated under the nickname "THAT'S ALL --- BROTHER." Fitted with extra navigational and radar equipment, this Skytrain served as a pathfinder and was a lead aircraft on D-Day in Normandy, dropping paratroopers of the 101st Airborne Division at 0048 on June 6, 1944. Ultimately, the Commemorative Air Force acquired the plane and restored it to its D-Day markings. *Rich Kolasa*

On D-Day in 1944, piloted by Lt. Col. John Donalson, "THAT'S ALL --- BROTHER" was the lead plane and pathfinder for over 800 C-47s, which delivered over 13,000 paratroopers into the battle zone in Normandy. In June 2019, the newly restored "THAT'S ALL --- BROTHER" crossed the Atlantic and participated in the seventy-fifth-anniversary commemorations of D-Day, in England and Normandy. *Rich Kolasa*

The left side of the forward fuselage, cockpit enclosure, nose, and "THAT'S ALL --- BROTHER" nickname inscription are in view. Yellow markings around the entry door show where the aluminum-alloy skin could be cut to effect a crew rescue, should the door become jammed. *Rich Kolasa*

Douglas C-47A-65-DL, serial number 42-100591, is preserved in airworthy condition by the Valiant Air Command, Inc., Flying Museum, Titusville, Florida. Delivered to the Army on November 6, 1943, this Skytrain, nicknamed "TICO BELLE," served with the 84th Troop Carrier Squadron (hence, the code "Z8" aft of the cockpit), 437th Troop Carrier Group, Ninth Air Force. On D-Day, June 6, 1944, the plane towed a glider full of troops from the 82nd Airborne Division to a landing zone near Sainte-Mère-Église, Normandy. Later that summer, "TICO BELLE" participated in Operation Dragoon, the invasion of southern France. *Rich Kolasa*

"TICO BELLE," C-47A-654-DL, serial number 42-100591, is viewed from aft while taxiing. The white vane antenna atop the fuselage is a postwar modification. *Rich Kolasa*

"TICO BELLE" makes a landing approach. Following World War II, this C-47A served, successively, in the air forces of Norway and Denmark. *Rich Kolasa*

The antenna directly to the front of the astrodome on "TICO BELLE" is the VOR localizer, part of the instrument-landing system. The twin pitot-tube masts are visible below the cockpit. *Rich Kolasa*

Douglas C-47A-40-DL, serial number 42-24064, is another World War II Skytrain that has been restored to flying condition and wartime camouflage and markings. It was built at Long Beach and delivered to the Army on July 26, 1943. In Europe the plane served with the 74th Troop Carrier Squadron, 434th Troop Carrier Group, participating in campaigns from Normandy to the crossing of the Rhine River. The squadron's code, "ID," and the plane's call letter, "N," are present on the re-created markings. *Rich Kolasa*

Douglas C-47A-70-DL, serial number 43-30652, has been restored to airworthy status. Most recently, this plane was in the collection of the 1941 Historical Aircraft Group Museum, Geneseo, New York. In the re-creation of its wartime camouflage and markings scheme, it carries the "W7" code of the 37th Troop Carrier Squadron, part of the 316th Troop Carrier Group. The call letter on the tail is "R." *Rich Kolasa*

C-47A, serial number 43-30652, is observed from the left rear, with the passenger door on the forward panel of the cargo door open. Atop the vertical fin is a red, rotating anticollision beacon, a postwar modification. *Rich Kolasa*

The same C-47A, serial number 43-30652, is taking off, with main landing gear still fully lowered. The control surfaces are fabric covered and appear to be a lighter shade of Olive Drab than the adjacent metal surfaces. *Rich Kolasa*

In an in-flight view of the bottom of C-47A, serial number 43-30652, on the bottom of the center section of the wing are four rectangular panels, immediately above which are the four fuel tanks. *Rich Kolasa*

During a demonstration, paratroopers are jumping from this C-47A, serial number 43-30652. *Rich Kolasa*

The same C-47A, marked "W7*R," is wheels down on a runway, with flaps lowered. After World War II, this Skytrain flew with a number of airlines in the United States and Canada. *Rich Kolasa*

C-47A-20-DK, serial number 42-93096, was delivered on April 8, 1944, and flew pathfinder paratroopers to a drop zone at Sainte-Mère-Église, Normandy, as part of Mission "Boston" on D-Day, June 6, 1944. For Operation Market on September 17, 1944, the plane again fulfilled this role, transporting pathfinders to their drop zone in Holland. This Skytrain subsequently flew missions in other significant airborne assaults and missions until the end of the war. It is now on static display at the National World War II Museum, in New Orleans, Louisiana. *Author*

The aft fuselage and empennage of the C-47A displayed at the National World War II Museum are viewed from the front left. The passenger door cut into the forward panel of the cargo door is open. *Author*

The left engine, Hamilton Standard Hydromatic propeller, cowling, and nacelle of the National World War II Museum's C-47A are showcased. An excellent view is available of the twin pitot tubes, on separate, adjacent masts. *Author*

The front of the Pratt & Whitney R-1830 radial, air-cooled engine is visible inside the right cowling of the C-47A at the National World War II Museum. The propeller is a Hamilton Standard Hydromatic, with its distinctive dome shell on the hub. Atop the engine nacelle just aft of the cowling is the carburetor air scoop. *Author*

Many details are revealed in this photo of the underside of the left engine nacelle. At the center is the main landing gear, including the wheel, oleopneumatic shock-absorber struts, and yoke-type brace strut, the rear of which fits into a pocket in the nacelle when the landing gear is retracted. To the front of the wheel is the oil-cooler housing. On the outboard side of the nacelle is the engine exhaust, which incorporates a muff-type heat exchanger and an exhaust outlet. *Author*

An overhead view of the C-47A at the National World War II Museum shows the windscreen, right cockpit window, and, on the cockpit roof, the escape hatch. To the immediate rear of the hatch is a horseshoe-shaped AT172/ARN14 localizer-omni antenna, to the rear of which is another, curved antenna. *Author*

In October 1943, the Army requested that the design be changed to allow operation at increased altitudes. To do this, Douglas installed R-1830-90B engines equipped with a two-speed supercharger. The Army was pleased with the results, and a new model entered production, the C-47B. These were powered by further-improved R-1830-90C engines. The low-speed ratio of the supercharger on these engines was the same, 7.15:1, as on the R-1830-92 but had a high-speed ratio of 8.47:1. The low gear ratio allowed the engines to operate efficiently at sea level and low altitudes, while the high gear ratio allowed the engine to maintain higher power at greater altitudes.

Essentially the entire power plant package had to be redesigned to accommodate the engine change, which entered production at aircraft 3986 and was accepted by the USAAF on June 24, 1944.

The supercharger-equipped aircraft were especially welcome to China-Burma-India (CBI) theater pilots because with the C-47B they could fly over "the Hump," the eastern end of the Himalayan Mountains, when heavily laden with cargo, rather than having to navigate a maze of passes as was required by prior C-47 models with similar loads.

Through contract amendments, C-47A aircraft contracted for at both plants but not yet begun were instead to be built as C-47B aircraft.

C-47B production at Long Beach was short lived, with only three hundred having been built, beginning with 43-16133, construction number 20599. The last of the type, C-47B 43-16432, construction number 20898, was accepted by the Army Air Force on August 31, 1944.

The Midwest City plant delivered its first C-47B, USAAF serial number 43-48263, in July 1944. That aircraft was procured on contract W-535-AC-40658. That contract, signed in June 1943, was originally for two thousand C-47A aircraft, but production had shifted to the B model before any of the aircraft on this order were produced; thus they were built as C-47Bs.

In February 1944, contract AC-2032 was awarded, calling for 1,600 C-47Bs to be built in Oklahoma. This contract was later modified to substitute 131 of a much-improved model, designated the C-117A, for a like number of C-47Bs.

This contract was followed four months later with what was to be the last C-47 contract, AC-2989. The aircraft on this contract were scheduled for delivery in 1947. On VE-Day, marking the Allied victory in Europe, the 4,766th C-47 rolled off the Oklahoma assembly line. With that, and coupled with rapid gains against Japan, on May 25, 1945, the government announced that C-47 production would gradually taper down through December, and that 1946 production would be set at about half that of originally scheduled.

The headline of the *Daily Oklahoman* on Sunday, August 17, 1945, read, "12,000 Douglas Jobs End Today." The underlying story stated that "Oklahoma City was brought face to face with its first big problem of reconversion Thursday with the discharge of 12,000 Douglas workers following cancellation of contracts for production of the famous C-47 transports." The article went on to state, "The city plant has built 5,355 transports in its 33½ months of operation." The same paper, the day prior, had reported, "At the peak, in September 1944, Douglas C-47s were rolling off at thirteen-a-day clip, and production held at twelve-a-day until early this year, when tapering to the present six-a-day began. Skytrain No. 5,355 rolled off the line VJ-Day."

Production of the aircraft, as with most government contracts, would be terminated at the point deemed to be most economical. On VJ-Day, there were 131 C-47s and C-117s of contract AC-2032 on the line in various states of assembly. For contract 2989, this meant it was canceled entirely.

Just over a month later, on Friday September 21, 1945, the *Daily Oklahoman* again reported news from the massive Douglas plant, saying,

Sixty-six cargo and transport airplanes, which were in the final assembly and testing operations, will be completed by the Douglas Aircraft plant as a result of negotiations with the army air forces, Maj. D. E. Eggleston, AAF plant representative, announced Thursday.

Eight of the 66 planes are C-117 personnel transports, which will be completed for use of commercial airlines through a purchase agreement with the AAF, Pearson (plant manager) said.

The other 58 planes, including 53 C-47[-]type planes and five C-117s, will be completed for the air forces. The C-47s were off the final assembly line and in the final stages of completion on VJ-Day.

Pearson said he expects the work to be completed by November 1.

A follow-up story on December 18 provided slightly different numbers, stating,

All production at the Oklahoma City Douglas plant will be ended before January 1. . . . Since VJ-Day, August 17, Douglas has completed 47 C-47 cargo planes at the Oklahoma City plant and is winding up production of 45 C-117s, a lighter counterpart of the famed cargo and troop transport plane which was used in all theaters of the war.

Seventeen of the C-117s have go to the army and the remaining 28 are being produced for commercial transport use.

The final C-47 built in Oklahoma (Midwest) City was C-47B-50-DK, USAAF serial number 45-1139, Douglas construction number 34409, which rolled off the line on October 23, 1945. Interestingly, that aircraft, like many of the C-47Bs built in Oklahoma, through a clerical error, originally had another construction number assigned to it, specifically 17142.

Douglas Aircraft developed the C-47B as a high-altitude transport plane, capable of flying over the Himalaya Mountains in the China-Burma-India theater. To accomplish this, Pratt & Whitney R-1830-90 engines with two-stage superchargers were installed, to improve engine performance in the thin air above the mountains. This C-47B-1-DL in bare-aluminum finish is the first example of the model, serial number 43-16133. *National Archives*

The first C-47B, serial number 43-16133, is seen from the left side. Atop the engine nacelle is the long housing for a non-ram air filter.

Douglas C-47B-1-DL Skytrain, serial number 43-16133 and manufacturer's number 20599, is observed from the left rear. This Skytrain was delivered to the US Army Air Forces on or around June 24, 1944.

The first C-47B-1-DL is viewed from the front. In the postwar years, the plane was converted to a VC-47D VIP transport. During the Vietnam War, it was converted to an AC-47D Spooky gunship, serving successively with the 4th Special Operations Squadron and Detachment 1, 56th Special Operations Wing. On June 8, 1970, it was transferred to the Royal Laotian Air Force.

An example from the first production block of the B-model C-47s is making a cross-country flight: it is C-47B-1-DL, serial number 43-16255. The plane was in bare-metal finish. Interestingly, the tail number, 316255, is also painted on the top of the left wing. This plane was delivered in July 1944. *National Archives*

The same C-47B-1-DL is viewed from the aft-left quarter. Information about its service in World War II is not available. In 1962 it was taken out of long-term storage at Davis-Monthan Air Force Base, Arizona, and was delivered to the Spanish air force. As of 2022 the airframe was in storage at Peterborough Airport, in Ontario, Canada. *National Archives*

Oklahoma City–built C-47B-35-DK, serial number 44-77152, was representative of a later production block of B-model Skytrains. It was delivered to the Army near the end of World War II, on June 14, 1945, in Olive Drab over Neutral Gray camouflage.

The same C-47B-35-DK, 44-77152, is seen from the left side. During the Vietnam Conflict, this Skytrain was transferred to the Cambodian air force, later serving with the Royal Thai Air Force. It is preserved at Phitsanulok Royal Thai Air Force Base, Thailand.

C-47B-35-DK, serial number 44-77152, is observed from the left rear. This sequence of photos was taken on September 21, 1947, a little over three months after the plane was delivered to the Army.

The same C-47B-35-DK is seen from the front, with the tailwheel turned to the left.

Currently nicknamed "WHAT'S UP DOC?" and marked with the "3X" code of the 87th Troop Carrier Squadron, part of the 438th Troop Carrier Group, this C-47B-25-DK, serial number 44-76423, flies at low level during a demonstration. After delivery on February 24, 1945, this Skytrain served with the Royal Air Force. Later, it saw service with the French and then the Israeli air forces. *Rich Kolasa*

The restoration of C-47B-25-DK, serial number 44-76423, included nose art of Bugs Bunny with the nickname "WHAT'S UP DOC?" above it. Quilted soundproofing material is on the interior of the crew door. *Rich Kolasa*

Douglas C47B-5-DK, serial number 43-48608, was restored in 2008 by the Gooney Bird Corporation, under the nickname "BETSY'S BISCUIT BOMBER," and as of 2009 was based at Estrella WarBirds Museum, Paso Robles, California. *Rich Kolasa*

CHAPTER 4
Floatplanes and Glider Tugs

In many ways, the C-47 performed logistical miracles, getting often desperately needed supplies quickly to points near the front line. However, there were instances where suitable landing strips did not exist. One ingenious method to address this problem was advanced that would allow the aircraft to land on water. EDO Aircraft Corporation of College Point, Long Island, New York, manufactured a pair of sophisticated floats that were installed on C-47-DL 42-5671 in early 1943. The resultant aircraft was designated the XC-47C. At the rear of each of the 42-foot-long Edo Model 78-29 floats was a rudder, which moved in concert with the aircraft's rudder while on the water. It entered into an aerodynamic stall and crashed into Jamaica Bay, New York, shortly after takeoff during a test flight on Saturday November 13, 1943.

Each float of the 5-foot, 8-inch-wide floats contained fourteen watertight compartments and a 325-gallon fuel tank. Each float also contained a main landing gear as well as a small nose landing gear, which was fully retractable.

Tests indicated that performance of the aircraft, not surprisingly, was hampered by the presence of the floats, and that the aircraft did not take off or land well on choppy water. While only one XC-47C aircraft was created, EDO did build more sets of floats, with various sources giving the quantities produced in the range of thirty-two to one hundred. There is evidence that in addition to 42-5671, floats were also installed on 41-18582, 42-92577, 42-92699, and 42-108868, with at least one, C-47A-10-DK 42-92577, surviving the war and being sold as surplus at Walnut Ridge, Arkansas.

Of course, another way to deliver goods without having to be concerned about the takeoff roll after delivery is by glider. Work to adapt the C-47 into a towplane began in mid-April 1942, and after extensive study of the C-47 fuselage structure, it was determined that after relatively minor modifications the aircraft would be a suitable tug, and a subsequent study was made to rig a tow attachment to the rear of the aircraft. Beginning in September 1942, the C-47 was equipped to serve as a glider tug. Most often the glider of choice was the CG-4A Waco.

Quickly the Army determined that a strategy of using each glider for a single landing in enemy territory was wasteful, and techniques and equipment to use a C-47 to recover gliders were developed.

The mechanism was derived from a system created by Dr. Lytle Adams for the purpose of collecting mail along air-mail routes. His firm, All American Aviation, demonstrated an early unit, their Model 4, to the Army Air Corps in late summer 1941. In 1942, their Model 80 was introduced, which was tested the following year in a C-47. This system incorporated an improved braking system on the retrieval winch, which allowed the drum to accelerate without excessive loads, and subsequently to gradually stop. As a result, the system, which was installed on the left side of the cabin (6 feet aft of the cabin) and required a winch operator, could retrieve a glider with only 0.70 of a g-force, which lasted only six and a half seconds. This was far less force than a catapult launch from an aircraft carrier or even a rollercoaster. This was in part due to the use of nylon towropes, which would absorb much of the shock, even though the C-47 was flying 130 145 mph during pickup. Using this system, a glider could become airborne in as little as 60 feet, having accelerated to 120 mph (and the towplane decelerating accordingly). The winch was used to pull the glider from the 500-foot distance of pickup to much closer.

Further experiments proved that a C-47 could actually retrieve two gliders. Glider retrievals were used in Europe and the CBI, as well as from various CG-4A factories.

However, serving as a glider tug was not the only glider-related use of the C-47. The XCG-17 was essentially a C-47 bereft of its engines and was intended to be used as a large glider towed by a C-54 four-engine transport. The initial conversion was made in June 1944, and while initial flight test results were favorable, the XCG-17 did not meet the Army requirements for landing on unimproved fields. In January 1946, a second attempt was made to utilize a C-47 as a glider, this conversion being made at Nichols Field in the Philippines. Flight tests of this too were successful, but the plan was abandoned and the aircraft had its engines reinstalled.

A C-47C, serial number 42-5671, was converted to a prototype floatplane, designated XC-47C. It was equipped with twin floats manufactured by the EDO Corporation. EDO produced approximately 150 sets of these floats for installation on C-47s.

Two rocket packs were installed below the bellies of aircraft equipped with the EDO floats, for assistance in takeoff. Personnel are making adjustments to the left rocket pack on this aircraft.

The rocket-assisted takeoff units are being test-fired on the XC-47C. The beaching gear consisted of a small nosewheel and a larger rear wheel, and these units retracted into wells in the floats, which were equipped with doors to close off the bays when the gears were retracted.

The XC-47C is just feet off the water during a test of its floats. The EDO floats on this particular aircraft were the Model 78 Amphibious Float Gear. A rudder was on the rear of each float.

#6. DOUGLAS C-47 "SKYTRAIN" ON EDO MODEL 78 AMPHIBIOUS FLOAT GEAR

During a test flight, the XC-47C cruises high above the clouds. Two light-colored lines, with "DANGER PROPELLER" lettered between them, were on the floats below the propellers. Mooring bitts were on the upper front and upper rear of each float.

A Skytrain with EDO floats, presumably 42-5671, presents its front to the camera, showing the designs of the forward "V" struts, which were nearly vertical, and the rear struts, which were angled.

A Skytrain with EDO floats is marked "615" on the nose. Two steps were built into the leading edge of the rear strut of each float. A deicing boot is clearly visible on the leading edge of the left wing.

A C-47C with EDO floats is parked on a tarmac at the aircraft disposal center in Walnut Ridge, Arkansas. The complete tail number is illegible on the aircraft, but it begins "292." Under the rear of the left float is a small strut, to prevent the aircraft from rocking back on the floats. In the left background is a group of Douglas C-54 Skymaster transport planes.

On the basis of practices pioneered by the US Post Office Department in using aircraft to snatch mailbags in hard-to-access locations, the Army Air Forces developed a method of snatching gliders where no other means of retrieval were an option. For glider recovery, two posts, called stations, were erected to the oblique front of the glider, and a nylon leader (rope), attached to the glider on one end and fitted with a loop on the other, was carried out to the stations, which held the loop well up in the air. The pickup aircraft, a C-47, was equipped with a Model 80 pickup unit, the main elements of which were a winch, to operate a long nylon rope with a hook on the end, and a long, swiveling pickup arm, to manage the nylon line and the hook. The C-47 would fly over the site, grab the loop and leader, and thus haul the glider up into flight. Here, the recovery C-47 is approaching the retrieval station, pickup arm lowered, with a British Airspeed Horsa glider to the left, and one of the stations supporting the retrieval loop toward the right.

In the second image in the sequence, the C-47 has flown over the Horsa, and the hook on its pickup arm grabbed the loop at the end of the nylon leader. Grid lines were drawn on these photos, apparently for spatial reference.

The leader, now towed by the C-47, has pulled the Horsa glider up and into flight. A flight crew in the cockpit of the glider would control it until it was released from the C-47 tug.

A C-47 has just snatched the leader of the Waco glider in the foreground, and as soon as the line becomes taut, the glider will lurch into the air. The pickup arm is visible below the C-47's fuselage.

In a public demonstration of the glider pickup procedure, an RAF Dakota is flying, pickup arm lowered, over a US Army CG-4A Waco glider. The nylon leader for the glider is visible to its front.

The Douglas XCG-17 was an experimental glider, developed during World War II, which its designers intended to be towed by the Douglas C-54. The conversion was affected by removing the engines, fairing over the fronts of the engine nacelles with dome-shaped covers, and removing unnecessary equipment. The original landing gear remained. The one factory-converted XCG-17 glider, shown here while being towed, was based on C-47-DL, serial number 41-18496. One other XCG-17 was converted in the field, at Nichols Field, Luzon, Philippine Islands, after the war, in January 1946, using C-47B-1-DL, serial number 43-16229, as the airframe.

CHAPTER 5

C-47 in World War II

The USAAF utilized the C-47 in every theater of World War II, be it transporting personnel, evacuating the wounded, dropping paratroopers, towing gliders, or doing what its "C-" designator indicated: hauling cargo. Hundreds more performed similar service for the US Navy and Marine Corps; the RAF, RCAF, and RAAF as the Dakota; and the Soviet Union, China, France, and other nations.

Dwight D. Eisenhower, in his book *Crusade in Europe*, stated, "Four pieces of equipment that most senior officers came to regard as among the most vital to our success in Africa and Europe were the bulldozer, the jeep, the 2½-ton truck, and the C-47 airplane. Curiously, none of these is designed for combat."

USAAC/USAAF serial number	Model/contract
California	
41-7722/7866	Douglas C-47-DL contract AC15847
41-18337/18699	Douglas C-47-DL contract AC15847
41-19463/19499	Douglas C-47-DL contract AC15847
41-38564/38763	Douglas C-47-DL contract AC37398D
42-5635/5704	Douglas C-47-DL contract AC20669
42-32786/32923	Douglas C-47-DL contract DAAC-1043
43-30628/30639	Douglas C-47-DL; all to US Navy as R4D-1 BuNo 12393/1240
C-53 California	
41-20045/20136	Douglas C-53-DO 20045 MSN 4810, 20046/20136 MSN 4816/4906 20047/20050, 20052, 20057/20059 built as C-53B
42-6455/6504	Douglas C-53-DO
42-15530/15569	Douglas C-53-DO contract AC-1040-DA
42-47371/47382	Douglas C-53-DO
C-47A California	
42-23300/23346	Douglas C-47A-1-DL contract AC-20669
42-23347/23355	Douglas C-47A-5-DL contract AC-20669
42-23356/23379	Douglas C-47A-10-DL contract AC-20669
42-23380/23412	Douglas C-47A-15-DL contract AC-20669
42-23413/23537	Douglas C-47A-20-DL contract AC-20669
42-23538/23580	Douglas C-47A-25-DL
42-23581/23787	Douglas C-47A-30-DL contract AC-20669
42-23788/23962	Douglas C-47A-35-DL contract AC-20669
42-23963/24085	Douglas C-47A-40-DL contract AC-20669
42-24086/24136	Douglas C-47A-45-DL
42-24137/24321	Douglas C-47A-50-DL
42-24322/24337	Douglas C-47A-55-DL contract AC-20669
42-24338/24419	Douglas C-47A-60-DL contract AC-20669
42-32924/32935	Douglas C-47A-DL contract DA-AC-1043
43-15033/15432	Douglas C-47A-80-DL Skytrain
43-15433/15632	Douglas C-47A-85-DL Skytrain
43-15633/16132	Douglas C-47A-90-DL Skytrain
Oklahoma	
42-92024/92091	Douglas C-47A-DK contract AC-28405 MSNs beginning with 11779 ranging to 11853, with MSNs ending with "8" skipped
42-92092/92415	Douglas C-47A-1-DK contract AC-28405 MSNs beginning with 11854 and ending with 12213, with MSNs ending with "8" skipped
42-92416/92572	Douglas C-47A-5-DK Skytrain
42-92573/92743	MSNs beginning with 12214 and going to 12387, with MSNs ending with "8" skipped Douglas C-47A-10-DK Skytrain MSNs beginning with 12389 and ending with 12577, with MSNs ending with "8" skipped
42-92744/92923	Douglas C-47A-15-DK Skytrain MSNs beginning with 12579 and ending with 12777, with MSNs ending with "8" skipped
42-92924/93283	Douglas C-47A-20-DK Skytrain MSNs beginning with 12779 and ending with 13177, with MSNs ending with "8" skipped
42-108794/108800	Douglas C-47A-DK Skytrain contract AC-28405 MSN 11788 to 11848, with only numbers ending in "8" in between
42-108801/108836	Douglas C-47A-1-DK S contract AC-28405 MSN 11858 to 12208, with only numbers ending with "8" in between.
43-47963/48262	Douglas C-47A-30-DK MSN 25224/25523 (originally allocated MSN 13779/14078)
C-47B	
43-16133/16432	Douglas C-47B-1-DL MSN 20599/20898 California
43-48263/48562	Douglas C-47B-1-DK Oklahoma MSN 25524/25823 (originally allocated MSN 14079/14378)
43-48563/48912	Douglas C-47B-5-DK MSN 25824/26173 (originally allocated MSN 14379/14728)
43-48913/49262	Douglas C-47B-10-DK MSN 26174/26523 (originally allocated MSN 14729/15078)
43-49263/49612	Douglas C-47B-15-DK MSN 26524/26873 (originally allocated MSN 15079/15428)
43-49613/49962	Douglas C-47B-20-DK MSN 26874/27223 (originally allocated MSN 15429/15778)
44-76195/76524	Douglas C-47B-25-DK
44-76525/76854	Douglas C-47B-30-DK
44-76855/77184	Douglas C-47B-35-DK
44-77185/77294	Douglas C-47B-40-DK
45-876/1048	Douglas C-47B-45-DK
45-1049/1139	Douglas C-47B-50-DK
45-1140	Douglas C-47B MSN 34410; to USAAF in Nov. 1945
45-1141/2544	Douglas C-47B MSN 34411/35814; contract canceled
C-53/R4D-3	
41-20045/20136	Douglas C-53-DO W-535-AC-18393, June 1941 20047/20050, 20052, 20057/20059 built as C-53B
42-6455/6504	Douglas C-53-DO, Sept. 1941
42-15530/15569	Douglas C-53-DO contract AC-1040-DA Jan. 42
42-15870/15894	Douglas C-53-DO contract DAAC-1047 Feb. 42
42-47371/47382	Douglas C-53-DO MSN 7313/7324
43-2018/2021	Douglas C-53C MSN 4964/4967 DC-3s intended for the airlines impressed off the production line by USAAF
43-2022/2034	Douglas C-53C MSN 4969/4980, 6346, 6347 aircraft ordered by the airlines but taken over by the USAAF while under construction
43-14404/14405	Douglas C-53 DC-3s impressed by USAAF from Pan American
43-36600	Douglas C-53 DC-3A-408 MSN 4809, ex-NC3000
C-53D	
42-68693/68851	Douglas C-53D-DO Skytrooper contract AC-26937
R4D series	
01648/01649	Douglas R4D-1 Navy equivalent of C-47
01977/01990	Douglas R4D-1 Navy equivalent of C-47 3131-3143 R4D-1 Douglas from Army
05051/05072	Douglas R4D-1 Navy equivalent of C-47
05073/05084	Douglas R4D-3 C-53s transferred from USAAF
06992/06999	Douglas R4D-3 C-53s transferred from USAAF
07000/07003	Douglas R4D-4 DC-3As taken over by US Navy from Pan Am
12393/12404	Douglas R4D-1 C-47s from USAAF contract (ex-43-30628/30639)
12405/12446	Douglas R4D-5 C-47As transferred from USAAF; redesignated C-47H in 1962

Douglas C-53-DO, serial number 42-15553, marked "48" aft of the cockpit canopy, is parked with US Navy PBY Catalinas and a Consolidated C-87 at Karachi Air Base, in Karachi, India (now Pakistan), on December 26, 1942. A red, white, and blue flash is on the vertical tail below the tail number. Subsequently, this C-53, which had been delivered to the Army on September 6, 1942, would see extensive service in North Africa. After World War II, it served with several airlines before being broken up by April 1973.

Although the C-53s were intended to carry troops instead of cargo, they sometimes were put to use transporting supplies. Pan American Airlines flew this C-53-DO, serial number 41-20092, under a contract with the US Army Air Transport Command, along a route from Miami, Florida, to South America in World War II, bringing personnel and supplies to ATC's bases in the Caribbean. In this November 1942 view, the Air Transport Command insignia can be seen on the fuselage to the rear of the passenger door.

While taxiing on soft ground at a base in North Africa on December 26, 1942, the right landing gear buckled on Douglas C-53-DO, serial number 42-15535. Subsequently, engineers recovered the aircraft, which was repaired and returned to service. A letter "G" is marked on the fuselage aft of the national insignia.

The nickname "SCARLETT O'HARA" is marked below the cockpit windows of this C-53-DO, serial number 42-6478, taking off from Berteaux Airfield, Algeria, on January 31, 1943. The Skytrain was carrying fighter pilots on the first leg of their trip back to the United States, where they would teach new pilots their craft. This aircraft was subsequently loaned to the RAF, who outfitted it for use by Air Marshall Sir Arthur Tedder.

Paratroopers are assembled around a group of Douglas C-47s at an unidentified base. A lone Martin B-26 Marauder is parked in the background. In the left foreground is C-47-DL, serial number 41-18679. The photo was taken after that aircraft's date of delivery, December 2, 1942, but probably before late June or early July 1943, by which point the national insignia on these C-47s, white star on blue circle, was changed. Most of the C-47s have para-packs mounted under their bellies: these were supply packs fitted with parachutes, for dropping supplies to ground troops. *National Archives*

This photo is a companion photo to the preceding one, very likely taken on the same date and at the same base, on the basis of the consecutive negative numbers. Some of these C-47s have swatches of a light-colored material taped to the sides of the fuselages near the cargo doors. *National Archives*

At an unidentified air base, a tractor with a trailer full of shipping boxes has been parked next to Douglas C-47A-90-DL, serial number 43-15972. The tail number, 315972, has also been stenciled in yellow on the left wing. The ailerons have a two-tone, wavy paint pattern. After World War II, this C-47A flew with a succession of private firms and was still in service as recently as 2011. *National Archives*

A formation of Marine Corps Douglas R4D-1s from the South Pacific Combat Air Transport Command is reportedly on a mission from Bougainville to Green Island. The first fully visible R4D-1 has the number "81" painted in a dark color with a light-colored border on the fuselage, forward of the national insignia, and on the engine nacelle, while the farthest plane has "69" on both of those locations.

Australian soldiers are loading used Allison V-1710 aircraft engines into a C-47 assigned to the Directorate of Allied Air Transport, at Ward's Drome, Port Moresby, New Guinea, on April 25, 1943. These power plants were to be flown to Brisbane, Australia, where they would be repaired and overhauled for further service. *National Archives*

In a photo taken on the same occasion as the preceding one, Australian troops manhandle an Allison engine into the main cabin of a C-47 at Ward's Drome. *National Archives*

Australian troops are unloading supplies from C-47-DL, serial number 41-18697, at Wau, New Guinea, on April 27, 1943; the supply flight had originated in Port Moresby, New Guinea. This Skytrain, which had been delivered to the US Army Air Forces on December 4, 1942, was assigned to the 6th Troop Carrier Squadron, 374th Troop Carrier Group, US Fifth Air Force, on January 12, 1943. *National Archives*

As photographed from inside a Douglas Skytrain, the left wing of which is visible to the right, four C-47s assigned to the 6th Troop Carrier Squadron, based at Ward's Drome, New Guinea, are on a supply mission to Wau, New Guinea, on April 27, 1943. *National Archives*

Douglas Skytrains from the 6th Troop Carrier Squadron, 374th Troop Carrier Group, are lined up and warming their engines at Ward's Point, Port Moresby, New Guinea, preparatory to a mission to transport supplies to a forward area in April 1943. Just to the left of center is C-47-DL, serial number 41-18660 and numbered "79" aft of the cockpit, nicknamed "Shanghai Lil." To the right is C-47-DL, serial number 41-38665, "86," nicknamed "Jayhawk 2nd," to the immediate rear of which is C-47-DL, 41-38659, number "84," "Miss Carriage." The plane numbered "89" aft of its cockpit window is C-47-DL, 42-32830. *National Archives*

A C-47-DL nicknamed "Swamp Rat," with a depiction of a slinking rat above the nickname on the nose, is prosecuting a supply mission from Ward's Drome to Wau, New Guinea, in April 1943. The Skytrain was serving with the 6th Troop Carrier Squadron. The number aft of the cockpit window is "62." *National Archives*

Paratroopers at an airfield in Tunisia are adjusting their gear before boarding C-47-DL, serial number 41-18341, bound for a drop zone in Sicily, during the Operation Husky invasion of that island in July 1943. Chalked on the fuselage next to the cargo door is "D-1." *National Archives*

Parachute infantrymen are making preparations for an airdrop in Sicily in the summer of 1943, alongside Douglas C-47A-DL, serial number 42-32924. This aircraft was delivered on March 4, 1943, and arrived in North Africa in May of that year. The white bars and red border on the national insignia were authorized for the brief period between June 28 and August 14, 1943. *National Archives*

During training maneuvers in 1943, a C-47, serial number 42-2484, is taking off from Comiso Airfield with a Waco CG-4A glider from the 52nd Troop Carrier Wing in tow. The glider was loaded with infantrymen, and the C-47 was carrying a full complement of paratroopers. *National Archives*

A C-47 and a Waco CG-4A glider under tow are observed from the rear as they take off from Comiso Airfield, in Sicily. The two aircraft were bound for Ponte Olivo, where, in a simulated airborne assault, the glider troops would land and the paratroopers would jump. *National Archives*

US Army Air Forces personnel watch from next to a Curtiss P-40 as a Douglas C-47 approaches for a landing at an airdrome in Italy on or around September 9, 1943. The first airfield captured in Italy was Monte Corvino, near Battipaglia, on September 11, 1943. Parked in the background are four C-47s, on two of which are visible RAF roundels on the fuselages.

An RAF roundel is partially visible behind the cargo door of a Douglas Dakota being loaded with cargo at the airfield at Cassibile, Sicily, on October 2, 1943. Visible atop the left engine cowling is a ram-filtered dust filter. In the left background is a Boeing B-17. *National Archives*

Douglas C-47s from the 433rd Troop Carrier Group are being prepared for their next mission, at the airfield at Lae, in Morobe Province, New Guinea, in October 1943. The Skytrain at the center is marked "382" aft of the cockpit. Partly visible in the left background is a B-25 Mitchell gunship.

A C-47A nicknamed "SANDY," from the 433rd Troop Carrier Group, is being fueled at Lae, New Guinea, in October 1943. Also present is the name "THELMA" on the left engine cowling. The nomenclature and data stencil below the cockpit window is partially legible; the serial number of the aircraft was 42-2372x, the last digit being smudged, but likely "5."

Nicknamed "SURE SKIN," Douglas C-47A-35-DL, serial number 42-23860, is flying a low-level supply mission to the 348th Fighter Group at Finschhafen, New Guinea, on December 18, 1943. At the time, this plane was assigned to the 68th Troop Carrier Squadron, 433rd Troop Carrier Group, Fifth US Air Force.

A C-47 nicknamed "CHASTITY CHARIOT" and numbered "256" is being serviced at an airfield in the China-Burma-India theater. Previously, this plane had served as a Dakota I in the Royal Air Force, but after being repatriated to the US Army Air Forces, it, by some accounts, was the first USAAF C-47 to see service in the CBI theater. The aircraft, seen here still wearing RAF camouflage, was assigned to the 1st Ferry Group and flew the "Hump" in 1942 and 1943.

Members of the 5th Indian Division are maneuvering a jeep into a Douglas Dakota Mk. III from No. 194 Squadron, RAF, during the reinforcement of the Imphal Garrison in Burma. Before being transferred to the RAF, this plane was Douglas C-47A-10, serial number 42-92668. Both the roundel and the tail flash were composed of dark blue and medium blue; the usual red-and-white elements of the roundel were deleted, to prevent friendly forces from mistaking the red circle for a Japanese *hinomaru.*

Douglas C-47-DL, serial number 42-32836, served as "Ambulance Plane #1" of the 803rd Medical Air Evacuation Squadron, USAAF, in the CBI. According to some accounts, this was the first ambulance plane financed by US war bonds. The nickname "Smilin' Jack" (the name of a comic-strip pilot) was painted in script below the cockpit side window, and large red-cross insignia were on the top and sides of the fuselage. This photo was taken in China on January 26, 1944. "Smilin' Jack" crashed upon takeoff at New Delhi, India, on May 27, 1945, and was written off. *National Archives*

Paratroopers of the 101st Airborne Division are readying themselves for the flight across the Channel to Normandy, on June 5, 1944, D-Day minus 1. Next to them is their transport, C-47A-10-DK, serial number 42-92717. The plane is marked with the "BY" code for the 98th Troop Carrier Squadron, part of the 440th Troop Carrier Group. For its assigned sortie, code-named Mission Albany, this C-47A was equipped as a pathfinder and carried extra SCR-717 navigation and radar gear. The assigned drop zone on the night of June 5–6 was near Sainte-Mère-Église.

Troops are pushing a trailer full of equipment into a C-47A-90-DL, serial number 43-15677, of the 9th Troop Carrier Command at a base in England on D-Day, June 6, 1944. The call letter "T" is on the tail. On the C-47s to the rear is the "ID" squadron code of the 74th Troop Carrier Squadron, 434th Troop Carrier Group, part of the 52nd Troop Carrier Wing. *National Archives*

On each side of the mass of aircraft in this aerial photo, taken on or just before D-Day, June 6, 1944, is a long line of C-47s from the 72nd Troop Carrier Squadron, 434th Troop Carrier Group. Between the C-47s are two similarly long lines of Airspeed AS.51 Horsas, British gliders that the US Army acquired through reverse Lend-Lease. The C-47s are marked with the 72nd TCS's unit code, "CU," in large letters aft of the cockpits. A single-letter code is on the tail of each C-47, and those planes, as well as the Horsas, have black and white "invasion stripes" on the wings and the fuselages.

Two columns of C-47s are warming their engines, with two columns of Waco CG-4A gliders between them, at a base in England on June 6, 1944, the first day of the invasion of Normandy. The code "M2" on the fuselages of the C-47s identifies the aircraft as part of the 88th Troop Carrier Squadron, 438th Troop Carrier Group.

Douglas C-47s bearing the "4U" code of the 89th Troop Carrier Squadron, 438th Troop Carrier Group, are preparing for takeoff for a mission to Normandy, at RAF Aldermaston, in Berkshire, England, on D+1, June 7, 1944.

Nicknamed "Wing Tip Willy," C-47A-25-DK, serial number 42-93730, from the 96th Troop Carrier Squadron, 440th Troop Carrier Group, Twelfth Air Force, is carrying paratroopers during the Allied invasion of southern France in August 1944. The squadron code, "6Z," is emblazoned on the forward fuselage; "R" is above the tail code. Above the forward passengers' windows is a scoreboard with mission markings.

The 436th Troop Carrier Group of the Ninth Air Force operated in the Normandy Campaign and, later, in Operation Market Garden, in Holland, but in August 1944 the group detached forty-nine C-47s to support Operation Dragoon: the Allied invasion of southern France. Two of those aircraft were photographed while transporting paratroopers to a drop zone during that operation, on August 15. The "U5" unit code for the 81st Troop Carrier Squadron is on both aircraft. In the foreground is C-47A-90-DL, serial number 43-15661, to the side of which is C-47A-65-DL, serial number 42-100550.

A C-47 from IX Troop Carrier Command, Ninth US Air Force, is about to drop supplies to friendly forces along an airstrip on the Cherbourg Peninsula in the summer of 1944. Parachutes carrying supplies, just dropped by another C-47, are visible to the upper right.

52035 A C

GIs from the 439th Troop Carrier Group are unloading cargo from a C-47 at an air base in France on September 6, 1944. The liquid container is a captured German jerry can, full of gasoline.

The Pathfinders were paratroopers who were dropped on a zone about thirty minutes before the main airborne force arrived, in order to establish and mark the drop zone. To assist with navigating the Pathfinders' C-47s to the drop zone, some of the planes were equipped with SCR-717C ground-mapping (also called "bombing through overcast") radar. Pathfinder planes often were painted matte black, to camouflage them in the night sky. This C-47, from the 36th Troop Carrier Squadron, 316th Troop Carrier Group, has a radar pod under its belly. It was photographed over France on a mission to Holland on September 8, 1944. The squadron code, "6E," is on the forward fuselage, and the aircraft's call letter, "D," is on the vertical tail.

Eight Douglas C-47 Skytrains, reportedly assigned to the 317th Troop Carrier Group, are flying toward a drop zone in the Southwest Pacific around the fall of 1944. While based in New Guinea in September 1943, the 317th participated in the first airborne operation in the Southwest Pacific, at Nadzab, New Guinea. The group was reposted to the Philippines in November 1944, where it provided logistical support to US ground troops and Filipino guerrillas.

Camouflaged Dakota IIIs (the British version of the C-47A) assigned to No. 267 "Pegasus" Squadron, Royal Air Force, are assembled at an air base in Italy during 1944. A representation of the squadron's symbol, Pegasus, the mythical winged horse, is visible below the side window of the cockpit on the first three Dakota IIIs. The serial numbers of the first two Dakotas are discernible: KG496 and FL589. The unit code "AI" is next to the roundel of the closest plane.

Douglas Skytrains and, to the sides, Waco gliders are lined up at an air base on November 14, 1944. A very close examination reveals that the squadron code on the forward fuselages is "7D," which was assigned to the 80th Troop Carrier Squadron, 436th Troop Carrier Group, which was based at Membury Airfield, between Bath and Reading, England, between March 1944 and February 1945.

Douglas C-47A-40-DL, serial number 42-24051, is part of a formation of Skytrains from the 73rd Troop Carrier Squadron, dropping supplies for the beleaguered defenders of Bastogne, Belgium, on December 23, 1944. Airdrops such as this one helped the defenders, from the 101st Airborne Division, to hold out until they could be relieved by ground forces. *National Archives*

Burmese civilians observe the activities as C-47s from the Tenth Air Force deliver supplies to a recently completed airfield in northern Burma, in 1944. On the tail number of the closest plane, the first three digits are of a dark color, but the number very likely is 293769, representing serial number 42-93769, which was a C-47A-25-DK delivered to the Army on June 25, 1944, and assigned to the India-China Division of the Air Transport Command on July 17, 1944. The plane was destroyed in an accident while taxiing on September 21, 1945.

In support of the construction of a pipeline for transmitting gasoline from India to Allied bases in China, Chinese troops are unloading pipes from C-47B-1-DL, serial number 43-16197, at the airfield at Mangshih, in southwestern China, on January 18, 1945. This C-47B has markings of the 319th Troop Carrier Squadron (Commando), of the 1st Air Commando Group, including the question-mark insignia on the tail and diagonal stripes on the aft fuselage. *National Archives*

Douglas Dakota Mk. III, serial number FD857, from No. 267 "Pegasus" Squadron, Royal Air Force, is flying a mission over Greek islands in the Adriatic Sea in January 1945. The call letter "S" is to the front of the roundel, and the squadron's Pegasus insignia is on the forward fuselage.

A C-47 flying at very low altitude is dropping emergency K rations for members of the 151st Infantry Regiment, 38th Division, at the Mariveles airstrip on Bataan, Philippine Islands, on February 19, 1945. The 151st Regiment was battling its way up the east coast of Bataan to link up with the US Sixth Army.

In February 1945, the 1st and 2nd Air Commando Groups shuttled reserve troops from Palel, India, to Meiktila, Burma, to fight in the battle at the latter place. Gurkha troops are boarding C-47A-90-DL, serial number 43-15699, at Palel on February 27, 1945. This aircraft was lost on June 27, 1945. The apparatus on the side and bottom of the fuselage was for picking up and retrieving gliders in otherwise inaccessible locations.

One of the first planes to land on the captured airfields at Iwo Jima was this C-47 (or possibly a USN or USMC R4D). On D+12, February 31, 1945, wounded Marines are being situated in the main cabin of the plane, for medical evacuation. *National Archives*

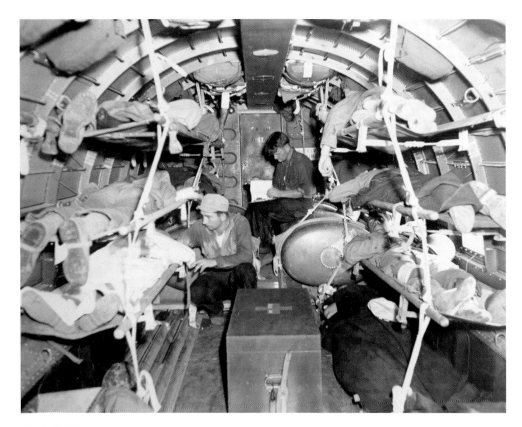

Two medics tend to seven litter patients (one of which is on the floor to the right) in the main cabin of the first C-47 to perform a medevac mission from Iwo Jima, on March 3, 1945. The photo was taken after takeoff, facing forward. In the background are two cabin fuel tanks. *National Archives*

Army Air Forces maintenance men have just finished installing a self-sealing gasoline tank in a C-47 from the 1st Allied Airborne Army, on March 23, 1945. This was in preparation for the launching of that army's landings along the Rhine River near Wesel, Germany.

At an airfield outside Limburg, Germany, C-47s are being used to transport gasoline to VII Corps, Third US Army, during the advance into Germany, on March 31, 1945. A mix of German and US liquid containers are arranged in groups on the field. The C-47 to the right bears the "M2" code of the 88th Troop Carrier Squadron, 438th Troop Carrier Group. *National Archives*

GIs are unloading gasoline cans from a C-47 at an unidentified air base in Germany on April 7, 1945. On the forward fuselage is the "Z8" code of the 84th Troop Transport Squadron, 437th Troop Transport Group. Above the forward passengers' windows is a scorecard of the missions this plane had completed. What appears to be shark's-mouth art is on the lower part of the nose. *National Archives*

Fuel drums for the advancing 3rd Army are lined up alongside C-47B-5-DK, serial number 43-48796. This Skytrain was assigned to the 321st Troop Carrier Squadron, 27th Troop Carrier Group. This squadron was one of a few that used a squadron code that had a fixed initial letter (in this case, "C"), and a variable second letter ("S" here), which was used to identify individual aircraft. *National Archives*

Airmen are unloading gasoline containers from C-47A-80-DL, serial number 43-15158, at a base in Germany on April 20, 1945. A variety of cargo—fuel containers, crates, and packs—is visible inside the cargo door. The "J8" squadron code on the C-47 to the right represents the 92nd Troop Carrier Squadron, 439th Troop Carrier Group. *National Archives*

In a test of a conveyor belt to discharge cargo, para-packs are dropping out of C-47B-25-DK, serial number 44-76230 and code 3D-T, from the 82nd Troop Carrier Squadron, 436th Troop Carrier Group, in France on April 11, 1945.

A litter patient is being transferred from an ambulance to a C-47, for medical evacuation, at Valencia Airstrip, Leyte, Philippine Islands, on May 12, 1945. At this time, C-47s would fly into Valencia with rations for the troops and then would evacuate wounded and ill GIs.

A Caterpillar tractor from the 40th Division Engineers is recovering a C-47A-70-DL, serial number 42-100724, which slid into a drainage ditch at Bacolod Airstrip, Negros, on May 18, 1945. *National Archives*

A local laborer is rolling a gasoline drum, with C-47A-25-DK, 42-93484, in the background. This aircraft, from the 318th Troop Carrier Squadron (Commando), 3rd Air Commando Group, was parked at the Laoag Airstrip, in Ilocos Norte Province, Luzon, Philippine Islands, in May 1945. The code "AO14" is painted to the rear of the cockpit.

"PRECIOUS INFANT" was a C-47 from the 318th Troop Carrier Squadron (Commando), based at Laoag, Philippine Islands. The aircraft was piloted by 2Lt. Harold R. Case, and the photo was taken as the plane was fueled prior to takeoff at Lingayen Airstrip. *National Archives*

A Douglas C-47 numbered "3678" on the nose is taking on fuel at Nichols Field, south of Manila, on Luzon, on May 31, 1945. A GMC 2½-ton 6 × 6 750-gallon fuel tanker is in the foreground. Fuel for aircraft at this airfield was supplied by the bulk petroleum plant at Nielson Field, Manila. *National Archives*

"CHARLOTTE M" is the nickname of a Douglas Skytrain, numbered AO18 aft of the cockpit, parked at the Lingayen Airstrip on Luzon on May 20, 1945. The plane was assigned to the 318th Troop Carrier Squadron (Commando). *National Archives*

Three Dodge ambulances have backed up, close to a C-47, to deliver battle casualties for medical evacuation, at an airstrip in Burma in May 1945. Within a few hours, these wounded soldiers would be receiving treatment at a military hospital. A red cross on a white background is visible under the left wing of the C-47.

A Dodge WC-54 ¾-ton ambulance has delivered a wounded US soldier to a Douglas C-47 from the 65th Troop Carrier Squadron for medical evacuation to Leyte General Hospital, in Tacloban, on June 15, 1945. The site was on the island of Negros, in the Philippines. *National Archives*

Part of a force of fifty-four C-47As from the 317th Troop Carrier Group, tasked with transporting elements of the 11th Airborne Infantry Division to drop zones at Camalaniugan, is lined up, awaiting orders for takeoff at Lipa Airstrip, in the Philippine Islands, on June 22, 1945. The nickname "JUNGLE SKIPPERS" is painted above the passengers' windows on these Skytrains. Codes painted aft of the cockpits of the first several planes, which are C-47As, include X6A, X13A, and X18A. *National Archives*

Part of the force of fifty-four C-47As seen in the preceding photo is viewed from another perspective, at Lipa Airstrip on June 22, 1945. Crewmen are relaxing on folding cots and litters underneath the planes. *National Archives*

Douglas C-47s loaded with troops from the 11th Airborne Division are approaching the drop zone at the Apari airstrip, in northern Luzon, on June 23, 1945. In addition to troops, these planes were carrying field artillery pieces, jeeps, and a trailer fitted with long-range radio equipment.

Some Douglas C-47s engaged in search-and-rescue operations were modified with clear blisters on the sides of the fuselage, aft of the wings, to give observers a better downward view. This example was installed on a C-47 used in Arctic search and rescue; the photo was dated February 27, 1945. *National Archives*

"RESCUE" is inscribed in large letters on the upper fuselage of Douglas C-47A-90-DL, serial number 43-16109. This Skytrain served with the US Army Air Force's 3rd Emergency Rescue Squadron in the Philippines during the final year of World War II. The last two passenger windows are bubble type, to provide observers with a wider field of vision.

CHAPTER 6
USAF

Following World War II, thousands of now-superfluous warplanes, including C-47s, were sold as surplus, with the C-47s typically garnering more interest, and more money, than other aircraft. In late 1946, a large group of C-47s and R4Ds were sold in Ontario, California, and Augusta, Georgia, with prices ranging from $15,000 to $22,500. These prices were significantly higher than the prices realized for combat aircraft, since the C-47 had obvious commercial value, whereas there was little utility in a surplus fighter or bomber. The surplus C-47s, along with veteran pilots leaving military service, would form the backbone of the post–World War II commercial aviation industry.

While some of the C-47s would go into service as a commercial cargo transport with little modification, others were converted to DC-3 configuration, which involved more-extensive changes.

The FAA issued guidance on such matters, which included "Passenger compartment capacity must be restricted to 22 persons unless a total of three emergency exits are installed. Most C-47 models have only two such exits."

The FAA also directed certain modifications, including "The following military equipment should be removed: Winterization (except oil dilution system and hopper oil tanks), propane priming, glider tow mechanism in the tail cone, litter boxes, litters, and supporting structure." Also, "If bullet sealing fuel cells are installed, the following must be complied with; Inspect the installation to ascertain that tanks are adequately supported, i.e., that tank, when empty, retains approximately its full shape and such that the weight of the fuel or cell will not cause sagging or pulling on any connections." The FAA also directed that "instrument markings and placards must be installed as required by this specification and commercial DC-3 practice. Attention should be given to the windshield equipment, and it should be determined that a satisfactory windshield wiper is installed." Further, if the aircraft had more than four thousand flight hours, the outer wing was to be removed and the wing attach angles and attach angle doublers inspected.

While large numbers of C-47s had been disposed of as surplus, either through sales on the civil market or transfer to allied nations, huge quantities remained in the US military's inventory when the National Security Act of 1947 became law on July 26, establishing the Department of the Air Force. The vast majority of the United States' remaining C-47 fleet became property of this new branch.

The two-speed supercharger utilized by the R-1830-90C engines of the C-47B were somewhat trouble prone, as well as being maintenance intensive. With the end of World War II and the advent of more-modern aircraft, the need for large numbers of C-47s capable of flying "the Hump" was somewhat abated. Thus, the Air Force undertook a modification program for many of the C-47B aircraft on the roster. The R-1830-90C engines were replaced with R-1830-90D engines, which featured only the single-speed 7.15:1 supercharger. R-1830-90C engines were converted to R-1830-90D configuration by removal of the two-speed clutch of the supercharger and installing a single-speed gear drive. Following the replacement of the -90C engine with the -90D, the aircraft were reclassified C-47D.

Following World War II, control of Germany had been divided between the Soviet Union and the Western allies, and Berlin, a city of two million, itself had been similarly divided, although the capital city was entirely within the Soviet-controlled portion of Germany. On June 24, 1948, the Soviets blockaded all road, rail, and water routes from the west to Berlin, as well as turning off electricity. This move cut off food and fuel supplies from the Western allies—the United States, United Kingdom, and France. However, earlier agreements had laid out specific air corridors as being under Allied control.

On June 26, the US launched Operation Vittles, and two days later the UK launched Operation Plainfare, both massive airlift operations. Initially, the US relied heavily on the venerable Gooney Bird, including the historic first mission. For the first several weeks, each C-47 involved in the operation flew three round trips per day. But during the course of the eighteen-month airlift, which

306476

In the postwar years, C-47A-35-DL, serial number 42-23918, was engaged in experiments with a rigid apparatus for towing a glider. As seen in a photo dated September 28, 1950, the C-47A is towing Waco CG-15A, serial number 45-5276, using a short tow bar. Markings on the C-47A, including "UNITED STATES AIR FORCE" on the fuselage and the national insignia with red bars, reflect the establishment of the US Air Force as a separate branch of the military on July 26, 1947.

required that 4,500 tons per day be moved (ultimately, over 9,000 tons per day were flown), it was increasingly supplanted by the Douglas C-54, which had treble the capacity as well as offering more-rapid loading and unloading. The final C-47 flight in what became known as the Berlin Airlift was flown in September 1948, and a year later, on September 30, 1949, the operation was discontinued, following the lifting of the blockade by the Soviets.

By the time that the North Koreans crossed the thirty-eighth parallel in June 1950, starting the Korean War, the C-54 had become the primary USAF cargo aircraft. However, there were only three C-54 squadrons, one in the Philippines and two in Japan, in June 1950. Accordingly, the Far East Air Forces ordered every C-47 in the area moved to Japan.

This proved wise since many of the Korean airfields could not support the large and heavy C-54, and as a result the C-47s were widely used bringing troops and equipment to Pusan. Thus, the C-47 began to reprise many of its World War II roles during the Korean War, with USAF and Royal Hellenic Air Force Gooney Birds flying numerous supply missions.

In September 1950, forty C-47s joined seventy-five C-119s in dropping paratroopers near Sukchon-Sunchon, the first airborne operation of the war. In addition, during the Korean War, C-47s were used as airborne radio relay stations, as well as to drop flares to guide night bomber attacks. Such uses were to be a glimpse into the future of the Gooney Bird.

When Soviet forces blockaded land routes into the Allied-controlled parts of Berlin in June 1948, the Allies quickly initiated an emergency airborne network to fly supplies into the encircled city. In a photo taken during the Berlin Airlift, USN Douglas R4Ds and USAF C-47s are lined up on the tarmac at Tempelhof Airport in Berlin, as supplies are unloaded from their main cabins. The nearest plane is C-47A-90-DL, serial number 43-15672.

Douglas Skytrains are observed from the terminal building at Tempelhof Airport during the Berlin Airlift. Semitrailers are backed up to the two closest planes, to take on cargo.

A C-47 flies low over East Berlin during Operation Vittles. During the most intense part of the operation, supply planes were landing every forty-five seconds at Tempelhof Airport. The airlift was a success, and on May 11, 1949, the Soviets discontinued the blockade of West Berlin.

German workers are unloading bags of flour from a Douglas Skytrain during the Berlin Airlift. The US supply mission during this crisis was code-named Operation Vittles.

On May 27, 1948, a C-47 in the service of the United Nations and the Red Cross is about to take off from Le Bourget Airport, Paris, to transport Folke Bernadotte, Count of Wisborg, a prominent Swedish diplomat, to Palestine, where he was to serve as United Nations mediator in Palestine. He was assassinated by Zionist terrorists in Jerusalem on September 17, 1948.

Douglas C-47B-5-DK, serial number 43-48765, displays the operation of a JATO (jet-assisted takeoff) apparatus from a muddy wheat field at Greenup, Illinois, on December 9, 1948. The pilot was Capt. James Doolittle Jr., from Wright Field, Ohio. *National Archives*

During the desperate Battle of Chosin Reservoir, in North Korea, in December 1950, Hagaru-ri became an important supply dump, with an airstrip, 1st Marine Division headquarters, and a direct-air-support center. Skytrains assisted in supplying this base. The one to the left has arrived with a load of supplies; a radio direction-finding loop antenna is on the bottom of the nose. To the right of that plane, a Skytrain is beginning its takeoff run. In the air to the right of center are over twenty parachutes, carrying supplies dropped from a C-119.

As the Army crew of an M19 multiple gun motor carriage guards the perimeter of an advanced air base 3 miles from Chinese Communist forces, a USAF C-47 takes off with a cargo of wounded GIs, bound for a hospital behind the front lines, in Korea around early 1951. Because of the proximity of enemy forces to the base, C-47 pilots flying to it received special briefings before their missions, so that they could avoid enemy fire. *National Archives*

At an air base in Japan, local laborers are laying down steel matting as a C-47 assigned to the 315th Air Division (Combat Cargo) takes off on a mission to transport supplies to United Nations forces fighting in Korea, in August 1951. A large number, "434," is marked on the fuselage aft of the cockpit. *National Archives*

80870 A.C

Douglas C-47B-15-DK, serial number 43-49548, from the 21st Troop Carrier Squadron "Kyushu Gypsies," 315th Air Division (Combat Cargo), is preparing to take off from a dirt airstrip in the mountains north of the thirty-ninth parallel, in central Korea, during 1952. The plane was going to transport wounded Marines to a base on the east coast of the Korean Peninsula, from which the casualties would be transported by helicopters to the Navy hospital ship USS *Consolation* (AH-15). *National Archives*

The honor of being the first aircraft to ever land at the geographic North Pole belonged to a Skytrain: C-47A-90-DL, serial number 43-15665. After serving with the 73rd Troop Carrier Squadron, 434th Troop Carrier Group, in Europe in World War II, this aircraft was selected to make the landing at the North Pole on May 3, 1952, as part of Operation Oil Drum. The photo shows the plane at the pole on that date, with skis mounted on the landing gears and "UNITED STATES AIR FORCE" marked above the passenger windows. Later that year, on November 3, the plane crashed on Fletcher's Ice Island, and it was never recovered.

C-47B-30-DK, serial number 44-76632, a Skytrain of the 21st Troop Carrier Squadron "Kyushu Gypsies," churns up a spray from rainwater covering steel matting during a takeoff run in September 1952. Aircraft of the Gypsies were leaving this unidentified base to weather out a hurricane at another base, in southern Japan. *National Archives*

The first Douglas aircraft designated AC-47 (as opposed to the later AC-47D gunship) were electronic-listening planes, converted from C-47Ds by Hayes Corporation in 1953. The AC-47s were packed with electronic monitoring sets, a weather-avoidance radar in the redesigned nose, and an array of electronic navigational and communications gear. These two AC-47s were assigned to the 1850th Airways and Air Communications Squadron of the Military Air Transport Command.

Some C-47s were completed as TC-47s and used as trainers for navigators. These aircraft were equipped with two extra astrodomes, in addition to the stock astrodome aft of the cockpit, for the use of student navigators in making celestial observations. This example, USAF TC-47B-5-DK, tail number 0-348641 and serial number 43-48641, was delivered on September 5, 1944; it was photographed flying over a coastline on June 27, 1956. *National Archives*

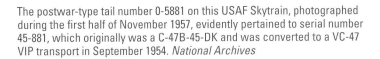

The postwar-type tail number 0-5881 on this USAF Skytrain, photographed during the first half of November 1957, evidently pertained to serial number 45-881, which originally was a C-47B-45-DK and was converted to a VC-47 VIP transport in September 1954. *National Archives*

Douglas C-47A-80-DL, serial number 43-15343, was converted to a VC-47A VIP transport in September 1954. It is seen here during service with the New York Air National Guard, parked at Wheeler-Sack Army Airfield, Fort Drum, New York, in August 1958. A thunderbolt design was painted along the side of the fuselage and on the vertical tail.

In John F. Kennedy's January 1961 inauguration speech, he said, "Let every nation know, whether it wishes us well or ill, that we shall pay any price, bear any burden, meet any hardship, support any friend, oppose any foe to assure the survival and the success of liberty." In October of that year, he turned those words into action by authorizing a USAF detachment be deployed to South Vietnam. That unit was the 4400th Combat Crew Training Squadron, later renamed the 1st Air Commando Wing.

This mission was given the name Farm Gate, and its stated purpose was to train South Vietnamese air force personnel in the use and operation of the aircraft that were going to be supplied to them by the USAF. These included the B-26 Invader, the T-28 Trojan, and four C-47s. Operations in Vietnam began on December 19, 1961, with the first combat sortie on January 13, 1962.

C-47s had operated in the skies over Vietnam since World War II, first by the USAAF and the RAF during World War II, then by the French in the 1950s. During Farm Gate, in addition to the transport role, a special variant of the Gooney Bird, the SC-47, was used in the psychological-warfare operations. The aircraft dropped leaflets and messages boomed out of the massive cargo-door-mounted loudspeaker array, urging the North to capitulate. On March 11, 1962, SC-47D 44-76330, dropping leaflets, went down over Laos, taking six airmen, two US Army soldiers, and a Vietnamese air force observer with it, becoming the first Farm Gate loss. One of the soldiers, US Army major Lawrence Bailey, bailed out, survived, and became a POW.

In addition to the SC-47, the EC-47 was also used throughout the war. In fact, the final Gooney Bird lost in Vietnam was EC-47Q 43-48636, assigned to the 361st Tactical Electronic Warfare Squadron, 56th SOW, which was shot down in Laos on the night of February 4–5, 1973, killing all eight crewmen.

Arguably the most famed variant of the C-47 to see use in the Vietnam era was the AC-47 gunship. This highly lethal platform began evaluation operations in Vietnam in December 1964, after having survived years of delayed testing and development in the United States, and considerable resistance to the concept from many Air Force officers.

The test team, lead by Capt. Ronald W. Terry, arrived in South Vietnam on December 2, 1964, with the modification kits for installing GE 7.62 mm Miniguns being delivered a week later. The first modified aircraft, then termed FC-47, was ready on December 11, and a second aircraft was completed on December 15.

Training of crews, drawn from the 1st Air Commando Squadron, began immediately, and the first daytime combat mission was flown on December 15, with the first night mission being flown the night of December 23–24. The results of these missions exceeded the expectations of all involved. By December 26, 1964, the aircraft had flown sixteen combat missions as well as seven training missions and had fired 179,710 rounds of ammunition.

Word quickly spread of the effectiveness of the weapon, leading to a surge in demand. The Miniguns, a relatively new item with a long lead time for production, were already in demand as armament for helicopters. As a result, it was expected to take several months before more guns became available for installation in C-47s. As an interim measure, some C-47s were equipped with an array of ten .30-caliber side-firing machine guns. The FC-47s so equipped proved effective, but the barrels of already-obsolete guns wore rapidly.

In June 1965, the Air Force initiated a program to withdraw twenty-six C-47s from storage; fly them to Warner-Robbins Air Force Base, Georgia; and there modify them to gunship configuration, with each aircraft being equipped with three GAU-2B/A gun pods. Since that gun pod remained in short supply, it was authorized to substitute the SUU-11A gun pod if needed.

In September 1965, the FC-47 designation gave way to AC-47D, dubbed Gunship I. Ultimately, there were fifty-three AC-47Ds built, which served with the USAF until mid-December 1969. At that time, they were replaced by Gunship II aircraft, the AC-130A.

The transfer of the AC-47Ds to the South Vietnam air force ended the story of the aircraft's use by the USAF.

Marked with a large United States flag below the cockpit, this C-47 was the sole aircraft assigned to the Military Assistance Advisory Group (MAAG) in Saigon when photographed in October 1951. The MAAG Group for Indochina had arrived in country in September 1950, its purpose being to provide military advice and material assistance to the French forces fighting Communist forces.

Skytrains were serving in the conflict in Southeast Asia before the United States began its major strategic buildup in Vietnam, as the Republic of Vietnam Air Force (RVNAF) was supplied with quantities of Douglas C-47 transports by the early 1960s. Several formations of C-47 Skytrains serving with the RVNAF are viewed from the rear during a mission in 1962 or 1963. They all are in unpainted aluminum finish.

The SC-47A was an air-search-and-rescue aircraft based on the C-47. The plane, which was redesignated HC-47A in 1962, was equipped with inflatable life rafts; waterproof, battery-operated radios; food and water; flares; and other specialized equipment. This SC-47A, originally C-47A-90-DL, serial number 43-15732, was photographed on October 22, 1955.

Nicknamed the "Gooney Bird" by its crews, the SC-47As performed a number of tasks, including transporting supplies to forward Air Rescue Service bases, dropping pararescue personnel in hard-to-reach locales, and dropping MA-1 (ARK) air-rescue kits to survivors on the ocean. This example, photographed at an advanced base in Korea, has markings on the nose for Flight C, 1st Air Rescue Squadron, Air Rescue Service.

An SC-47A flying over mountainous terrain in Alaska has a large "RESCUE" emblazoned over a yellow background. The tail number is 5894. A clear observation blister is below the "E" in the "RESCUE" inscription.

HC-47A (as the SC-47A was redesignated in 1962), serial number 42-92111, was converted to an SC-47A in September 1952. It served with the 1st Air Commando Wing in 1965 and was engaged in psychological-warfare operations in Vietnam in 1967. The plane is seen here, in Southeast Asia camouflage, taking off on a mission from Phù Cát Air Base, Republic of Vietnam, on June 26, 1971.

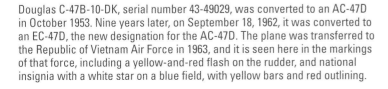

Douglas C-47B-10-DK, serial number 43-49029, was converted to an AC-47D in October 1953. Nine years later, on September 18, 1962, it was converted to an EC-47D, the new designation for the AC-47D. The plane was transferred to the Republic of Vietnam Air Force in 1963, and it is seen here in the markings of that force, including a yellow-and-red flash on the rudder, and national insignia with a white star on a blue field, with yellow bars and red outlining.

The RC-47s were converted from C-47s to fulfill photoreconnaissance and electronic-intelligence (ELINT) roles. This RC-47D, serial number 43-48902 and tail number 0-48902, was photographed at Elmendorf Air Force Base, Alaska, en route to Vietnam on July 27, 1967. Nicknamed "Old Patches," this was the last aircraft of the C-47 family to be assigned to the Air Force Communications Service, and it was retired from the service in 1972.

Built as C-47A-85-DL, serial number 43-15668, in April 1944, this EC-47N was assigned to the 361st Tactical Electronic Warfare Squadron in the Vietnam War era. System X mast antennas are above and below the wing, and an antenna is trailing from the rear of the fuselage. A white VHF antenna is atop the center of the fuselage.

EC-47N, serial number 43-15979, served with the 360th Tactical Electronic Warfare Squadron "Antique Airlines," attached to the 8th Tactical Fighter Wing, at Ubon Royal Thai Air Force Base, Thailand, from 1970 to 1972. The "AJ" code for the 360th TEW Squadron is on the vertical tail.

The "AL" tail code on this EC-47N, serial number 43-15979, pertained to the 361st Tactical Electronic Warfare Squadron, 14th Special Operations Wing, based at Phù Cát Air Base, Republic of Vietnam, 1966–71. Six wire antennas are routed from the forward fuselage to the vertical fin; these were known as a "banjo array" and were associated with the QRC-346 communications-jamming (COMJAM) electronic-countermeasures suite. This photo was taken on September 10, 1970.

Another aircraft assigned to the 361st Tactical Electronic Warfare Squadron, 14th Special Operations Wing, at Phù Cát Air Base was EC-47P, serial number 42-93735, photographed on November 6, 1970. This plane has just two wire antennas from the forward fuselage to the vertical fin, and System X mast antennas are faintly visible above and below the right and left wing. Sections of the engine cowlings are on the tarmac to the left.

Converted from C-47A-20-DK, serial number 42-93161, this EC-47N is parked inside a revetment at Phù Cát Air Base on February 13, 1971. The tail number is 093161, with "093" in small black numbers. The curved antenna above the cockpit is the VOR localizer, for use in instrument landings.

Douglas EC-47N, serial number 42-108980, was converted from a C-47A-25-DK and served with the 361st Tactical Electronic Warfare Squadron, 14th Special Operations Wing, at Phù Cát Air Base, Republic of Vietnam. The photo was dated February 14, 1971.

The same plane shown in the preceding photo is observed from the left side at Phù Cát on April 16, 1971. Two whip antennas are mounted on the deck to the rear of the cockpit.

A final shot of EC-47N, serial number 42-108980, from the 361st Tactical Electronic Warfare Squadron, shows the aircraft cruising above Phù Cát Air Base during October 1970. The national insignia on the aft fuselage and the left wing are the small, low-visibility version, with the normal USAF colors of red, white, and blue.

Douglas EC-47P, serial number 43-48947, assigned to the 360th Tactical Electronic Warfare Squadron, was a conversion of a C-47B-10-DK that was delivered to the Army on October 4, 1944. It is seen during a mission over the Republic of Vietnam on April 9, 1970. The Southeast Asia camouflage on the plane consisted of tan, two shades of green, and, on the undersides, light gray.

EC-47P, serial number 43-48947, of the 360th Tactical Electronic Warfare Squadron is flying a mission from its home base of Tan Son Nhut Air Base, Republic of Vietnam, around April 1970.

This EC-47P, photographed at Phù Cát Air Base on November 4, 1970, originated as a C-47B-5-DK, serial number 43-48767. At the time, the aircraft was serving with the 361st Tactical Electronic Warfare Squadron "Mach Turtles," part of the 14th Special Operations Wing.

Another EC-47P assigned to the 361st Tactical Electronic Warfare Squadron was this example, serial number 45-1046, photographed at Tan Son Nhut Air Base in November 1970.

Maintenance personnel from the 361st Tactical Electronic Warfare Squadron are servicing the Pratt & Whitney R-1830 engine of EC-47P, serial number 44-76668A, at Phù Cát Air Base in November 1970. The radome is propped open, showing the antenna of the AN/APS-113 weather-avoidance radar set inside.

The EC-47Qs were equipped with more electronic equipment than the -N and -P models of the aircraft, including two additional electronics consoles. The R-1830 engines of the -N and -P models was replaced by the more powerful Pratt & Whitney R-2000 engines. This EC-47Q was photographed at Edwards Air Force Base, California, in January 1971. *National Archives*

An EC-47Q, likely the same one in the preceding photo, is bristling with antennas in a frontal view. This aircraft was a conversion of C-47B-25-DK, serial number 44-76304, which was delivered to the Army on February 7, 1945. *National Archives*

Douglas EC-47Q, serial number 44-76304 and tail number 0-76304, is observed from the right rear at Edwards Air Force Base in January 1971. *National Archives*

Douglas EC-47Q, serial number 43-15681, served with the 360th Tactical Electronics Warfare Squadron in the Vietnam War, being based successively at Tan Son Nhut Air Base, Republic of Vietnam, and Nakhon Phanom Royal Thai Air Base, Thailand. At the conclusion of its service in Southeast Asia, the plane was flown to Clark Air Base, in the Philippines, where it was photographed on June 28, 1974. The plane was broken up at Clark Air Base on September 30, 1974.

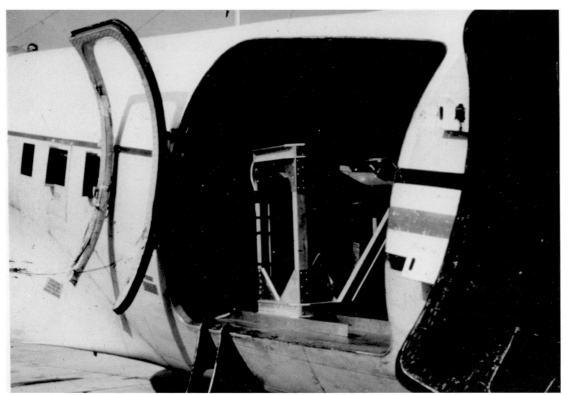

In the early 1960s, the US Air Force began a study of the efficacy of mounting side-firing guns in aircraft, which, when combined with flying the plane in a pylon turn over a target, could bring a highly concentrated, accurate, and sustained fire on the enemy. In September 1964, tests were conducted at Eglin Air Force Base, Florida, with a C-47 armed with side-firing General Electric GAU-2B/A Miniguns, a 7.62 mm rotary-barrel weapon with a rate of fire up to six thousand rounds per minute. The results were very good, and soon a number of C-47s were converted to AC-47D gunships. As a class, they carried the nicknames "Puff the Magic Dragon" and "Spooky." An inscription on this photo identifies it as "AC-47 prototype," showing the mounting stand for a Minigun inside the cargo door. The frame for the forward cargo door, with the passenger-door insert removed, is open; this frame would be omitted on subsequent AC-47s.

In a photo dated November 24, 1965, an AC-47D, serial number 43-48471, sports the white and aluminum paint it wore when it was converted to a gunship. Later, most AC-47Ds would be painted in Southeast Asia camouflage, either with black or light gray undersides. This plane was written off on February 18, 1968, following an accident during takeoff in Saigon.

The same AC-47D depicted in the preceding photo is viewed closer, showing the metal air deflectors attached to the forward sides of the two rearmost passenger windows as well as the cargo door, inside which 7.62 mm Miniguns are emplaced.

The middle air deflector on the same aircraft is shown. The deflectors evidently were a feature employed early on, with Spookys later lacking these devices.

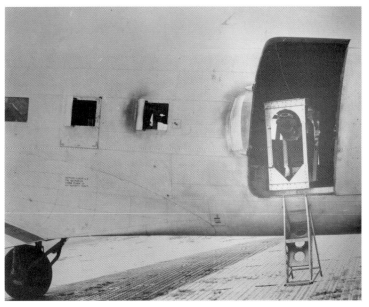

The Minigun is visible below the top of its metal stand in the cargo door of a Spooky. The air deflector for the door gun was about twice as tall as the two deflectors for the window guns.

Early on in AC-47D development, the SUU-11A and SUU-11A/A Minigun pods were used, being installed on metal stands, fastened to the floor. These pods were designed for installation on underwing pylons of attack aircraft. The Minigun pods in this Spooky are the SUU-11A/A type, fastened with three steel straps to the cradles of the stands.

Three SUU-11A Minigun pods are viewed facing to the rear of the main cabin. Jutting from the top front of each pod is a gun-support assembly. Various types of stands were used for the Miniguns; on the ones here, the pods are slung under the top of the stand. The pod contained linkless ammunition for the gun, as well as a control assembly and a battery for powering the Minigun.

The pilot of the AC-47D used a gunsight mounted inside the left-side window of the cockpit, for aiming the Miniguns while flying a pylon turn over a target.

The cargo-door-mounted Minigun of a Spooky is firing at a target on a hillside in Southeast Asia. The pods were mounted to fire slightly downward. Below the gun is an ammunition box, for collecting spent casings.

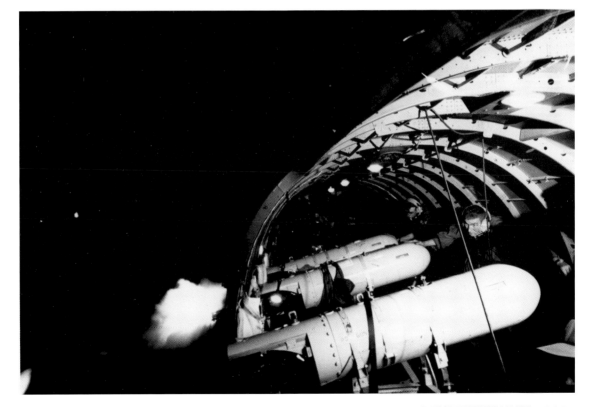

The center and, probably, the forward Miniguns of a Spooky are firing at enemy forces during a mission out of Pleiku Air Base, Republic of Vietnam, in November 1967. Although all three Miniguns could be fired at once, typically one or two were fired at a time. This was to have one gun on reserve in case one of the others jammed, and also, the recoil from firing all guns together caused the aircraft to slew to the right, affecting aim.

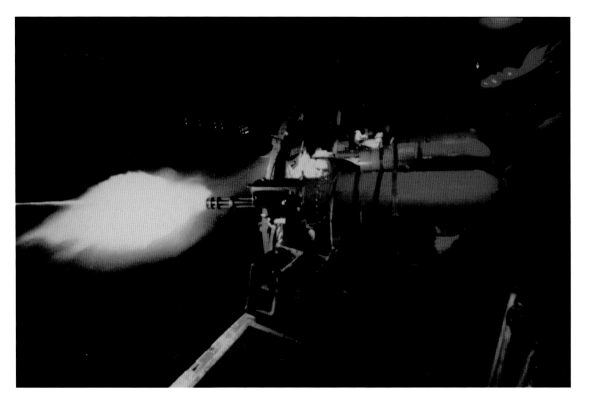

The aft Minigun is firing at a target during a November 1967 mission. The crew of the AC-47 typically included two gunners, to tend the Miniguns. Often included, in addition to the pilot, copilot, flight engineer, navigator, and loadmaster, was a South Vietnamese observer, who could communicate with Republic of Vietnam troops on the ground.

Each GAU-2B/A Minigun in a Spooky could fire at the rate of six thousand rounds per minute: or an astounding one hundred rounds per second! The maximum effective firing range of the weapon was 3,280 feet.

A Douglas AC-47D Spooky is parked at an unidentified air base in 1967. On this aircraft, the major part of the Minigun barrels is protruding through the two rearmost windows and the cargo door. A Skytrain, or possibly another Spooky, is parked in the background.

The Minigun barrels are in full view of a close-up photo of an AC-47D Spooky parked at Nha Trang Air Base, Republic of Vietnam, on January 23, 1967. This aircraft likely was a conversion of a TC-47 trainer, since the mountings for two astrodomes, a characteristic of that model of Skytrain, are visible atop the fuselage, aft of the standard astrodome.

Ground crewmen are loading flares onto an AC-47D Spooky, used on night missions to illuminate target zones. Flares are stored in a rack, visible inside the door. Initially, these aircraft carried thirty Mk. 6 parachute flares, rated at 750,000 candlepower, but later, forty-eight Mk. 24 Mod 3 parachute flares, with 2 million candlepower, were used. The loadmaster simply dropped the flares out of the cargo door when the pilot called for them.

SSgt. James P. Davis, a loadmaster on an AC-47D Spooky, is priming the fuses on parachute flares in their rack in the rear of the main cabin, in 1966. To his rear is an SU-11 A Minigun pod.

SSgt. Don G. Harrison, a loadmaster with Flight B, 4th Air Commando Squadron, is holding a Mk. 24 parachute flare in the main cabin of a Spooky, at Pleiku Air Base around April 1967. More flares are in the rack to his side.

Airmen are loading belted 7.62 mm ammunition into a AC-47D Spooky. The large main cabin of the aircraft enabled the Spooky to carry a very large amount of ammo for the Miniguns: 16,500 rounds were carried on a typical mission, but more could be stowed on board.

Around February 1967, Maj. Robert P. Knopf, commander of an AC-47D Spooky from Det 4, 4th Air Commando Squadron, is strumming the tune "Puff the Magic Dragon," a popular hit of the early 1960s and the namesake of the AC-47Ds. Maj. Knopf added his own lyrics to the original hit recorded by the trio Peter, Paul, and Mary.

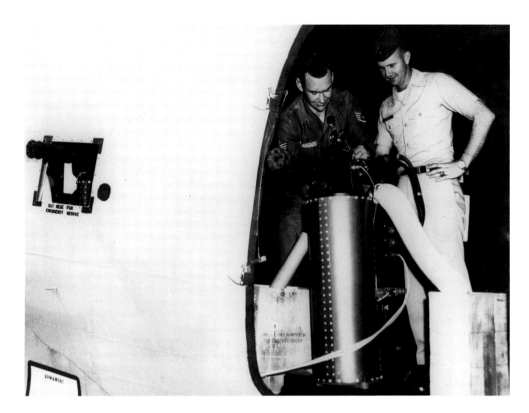

Eventually, the SUU-11 A and SUU-11 A/A Minigun pods in AC-47Ds were replaced by MXU-470 7.62 mm Minigun modules. On these units, the GAU-2B/A Minigun was mounted on top of a vertical drum containing two thousand rounds of linkless 7.62 mm ammunition. The drum could be reloaded automatically, using a power reloading mechanism, or manually by using a backup reloading system. In this undated photo, 1Lt. Ralph Kimberlin, *right*, and SSgt. George Thaggard are examining an MXU-470 in an AC-47D at Eglin Air Force Base, Florida.

Two window-mounted MXU-470s and a door-mounted one are lined up in an AC-47D at Eglin Air Force Base, Florida. The GAU-2B/A Miniguns could be fired at various rates, but three thousand and six thousand rounds per minute were the most commonly used ones. On the rears of the drums are control boxes. A spent-casing chute is on the side of the nearest drum.

In this configuration, the GAU-2B/A Miniguns of an MXU-470 module are pointing through the three rear passenger windows of an AC-47D, with the open cargo door visible to the far left.

On another FC-47D, four round firing ports have been neatly cut through the aft cargo door, to allow the barrels of AN/M2 .30-caliber machine guns (not yet mounted) to protrude.

Due to a shortage of Minigun pods early in the development of the Spooky, a few examples—sources differ on whether it was four or five—were armed with ten side-firing machine guns on the left side of the main cabin. These aircraft were designated FC-47D, "FC" standing for fighter-cargo. The machine guns were the Browning .30-caliber AN/M2, a variant of the M1919 .30-caliber machine gun, developed for aircraft applications in World War II. As seen on this FC-47D, two machine guns were mounted in each of the two rearmost passenger windows, two were inside the forward part of the cargo door (the actual door panel was removed), and four guns fired through openings in the aft cargo door.

Four AN/M2 .30-caliber aircraft machine guns are mounted on metal stands in the left side of the main cabin of an FC-47D, with two guns protruding through each of the two rear windows. The photo is dated March 1966.

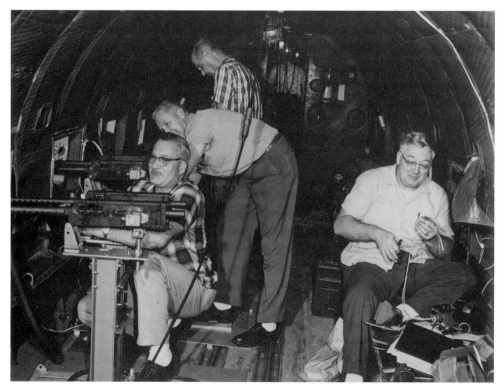

Civilian workers are mounting AN/M2 .30-caliber machine guns and assembling electrical components in the main cabin of an FC-47D in March 1966.

Douglas C-47A-25-DK, serial number 42-93791, is parked at McEntire Air National Guard Base, Eastover, South Carolina, on March 30, 1966. At that time the aircraft was assigned to the 157th Fighter Squadron, South Carolina Air National Guard, and evidently was serving as a squadron transport or VIP plane. On the tail, above the tail number, is stenciled "SOUTH CAROLINA" over the Air National Guard insignia. The finish of the plane was white over aluminum, with a black line dividing the two motifs.

Cruising above a Vietcong-held area on the coastline of the Republic of Vietnam, a USAF C-47 painted in Southeast Asia camouflage is dropping propaganda leaflets, as part of a psychological-warfare campaign to entice enemy fighters into surrendering. The photo was taken around the end of 1965 or the beginning of 1966. As a result of efforts such as this, reportedly some 1,600 Vietcong turned themselves in during that period, using the leaflets as safe-conduct passes.

A C-47 from an unidentified unit is parked at Albrook Air Force Base, in the Canal Zone, in 1967. The aircraft is painted overall in gray, with a matte black antiglare panel to the front of the windscreen. Deicer boots on the leading edges of the wings and vertical fin are black. A number is marked on the nose: "6379." *National Archives*

The same C-47 is viewed from the left rear at Albrook Air Force Base. The tail number, 0-16379, visible in this photo, marks this aircraft as C-47B-1-DL, serial number 43-16379. After service in World War II, from May 1956 onward it served with the 3110th Maintenance Group at RAF Burtonwood, UK, and with the 605th Air Commando Squadron in 1968. The plane was transferred to the Fuerza Aerea Dominica (Dominican air force) in 1972. *National Archives*

A C-47 with the tail number 92104 and serial number 42-92104 is flying over the ocean near Albrook Air Force Base, Canal Zone, in 1967. The plane is painted a light gray, with a white rudder. Delivered to the Army on August 1, 1943, this Skytrain served with the Massachusetts Air National Guard in the mid-1950s and later was assigned to the 605th Air Commando Squadron at Howard Air Force Base, in the Canal Zone.

Assigned to the 21st Composite Wing, an HC-47A search-and-rescue plane is parked on a tarmac at Elmendorf Air Force Base, Alaska, on March 16, 1967. The aircraft was painted white over natural aluminum, with high-visibility red paint on the nose, cockpit roof, and vertical fin. *National Archives*

A side view of the same HC-47A reveals its tail number, 0-23774, which corresponds to serial number 42-23774. Originally built as a C-47A-30-DL, this aircraft was delivered on June 4, 1943, and was converted to an SC-47A (redesignated HC-47A in September 1962) in the postwar era. Curiously, this plane has the original snub nose of the -47, rather than the elongated nose/radome of the HC-47A. *National Archives*

Douglas HC-47A, serial number 42-23774, is viewed from the left rear at Elmendorf Air Force Base on March 16, 1967. The wings and elevators were of aluminum finish. *National Archives*

The 21st Operations Squadron was the propeller-aircraft search-and-rescue component of the 21st Composite Wing, and presumably HC-47A, serial number 42-23774, was assigned to that squadron when this in-flight photo was taken near Elmendorf Air Force Base on March 10, 1967. *National Archives*

A Douglas C-47D marked with the tail number 0-49328, serial number 43-49328, is in flight near Randolph Air Force Base, San Antonio, Texas, in early 1967. This Skytrain has the long housings for non-ram air filters atop the engine nacelles. Built as a C-47B-15-DK, this aircraft was delivered in November 1944 and was transferred during the same month to the Royal Air Force, which designated it Dakota IV, serial number KK132. In the postwar era, the plane was converted to a C-47D. *National Archives*

The same C-47D, serial number 43-49328, is viewed from the lower left during a flight near Randolph Air Force Base in 1967. A study of photos of this aircraft reveals that there was a vertical mast antenna on the centerline of the bottom of the center section of the wing. *National Archives*

A Douglas C-47D is parked on a hardstand at Keesler Air Force Base, Mississippi, in April 1967. This plane has a vertical mast antenna underneath the center of the wing, and the bottom of a boarding ladder is visible below the passenger door on the left side of the fuselage. The lower parts of the plane appear to have been painted an aluminum color, rather than being bare aluminum. *National Archives*

Douglas C-47B-15-DK, tail number 0-49279 and serial number 43-49279, was spotted at Keesler Air Force Base, Mississippi, in April 1967. This plane reportedly was based at Keesler by 1960. This base was home to a number of USAF technical schools, and the unit crest on the vertical tail of this C-47B is that of Air Training Command. *National Archives*

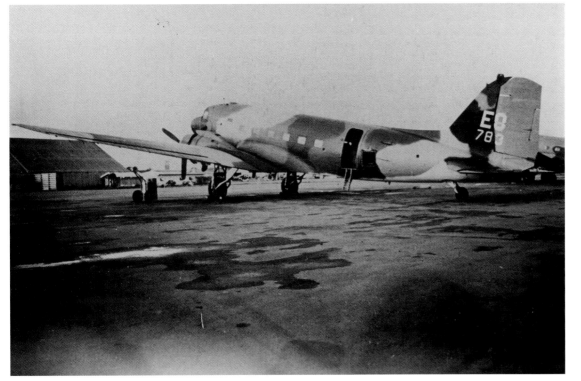

This C-47D served in psychological operations (PSYOPS) with Detachment (Det) 1, 5th Air Commando Squadron, and is parked at Bien Hoa Air Base, Republic of Vietnam, in mid-1967. The dark, square shape on the aft cargo door is a loudspeaker, for broadcasting messages to the enemy to surrender. The plane also had a chute for dropping leaflets. The C-47s of Det 1 also were equipped to drop Mk. 25 flares, to indicate targets for airstrikes or illuminate base perimeters at night. On the tail is the squadron's code, "EO," and part of the tail number is visible: 783.

A C-47D from Flight B, 5th Air Commando Squadron, is dropping leaflets over a Vietcong stronghold in an effort to induce the enemy to surrender, during a mission out of Bien Hoa in 1967. A loudspeaker is mounted in the aft cargo door.

During a daytime mission north of Pleiku, Republic of Vietnam, sometime before mid-January 1967, an AC-47D is firing its three Miniguns at enemy forces in the forest below. Smoke from the guns is streaming from the rear of the Spooky, and muzzle flashes are visible on the center and the rear guns. Visible inside the cargo door are the rear Minigun and the flare storage rack.

A VC-47A VIP transport, serial number 42-23793, of the Wisconsin Air National Guard was photographed on July 9, 1968. The plane was built as a C-47A-35-DL, manufacturer's serial number 9655, and was delivered on June 13, 1943. It was assigned to the Wisconsin National Guard in October 1947 and was scrapped in May 1972.

An AC-47D from C Flight, 3rd Special Operations Squadron, is parked at Bien Hoa Air Base, Republic of Vietnam, in July 1968. Below the side window of the cockpit is artwork of a ghost, in keeping with the plane's "Spooky" nickname. This ghost was also found on other AC-47Ds of that flight. On the tail in the background is the "EL" code of the 3rd Special Operations Squadron.

Douglas VC-47A-20-DK, another VIP transport, serial number 42-93172, was based at Forbes Field, Topeka, Kansas, when this photo was taken on August 20, 1968. The passenger door folded down and was equipped with handrails and steps on its inner side.

Painted in Southeast Asia camouflage, a C-47D, tail number 49495, is parked on a hardstand at Ubon Royal Thai Air Force Base, Thailand, in December 1968. Below the cockpit windows is cartoon art of a long-necked cat.

A photographer on the ground on the outskirts of Saigon captured this time-lapse photo of an AC-47D Spooky laying down a concentrated fire on enemy forces sometime in 1968. One out of every five rounds of 7.62 mm ammunition fired by the plane's Miniguns was a tracer, and these are what are visible as they stream from the aircraft to the ground as the Spooky makes a pylon turn over the target.

By the late 1960s, many C-47s were being placed in long-term storage at Davis-Monthan Air Force Base, Arizona. These Skytrains, including VC-47A (originally, C-47A-85-DL), serial number 43-15577, with markings for the Pennsylvania Air National Guard, are lined up at that base on January 10, 1969. Sealant has been installed over the windows, landing-light lenses, and access panels to protect them from the elements.

Details of the forward fuselage of VC-47A, serial number 43-15577, are in view in a photo taken on January 10, 1969. The sealant material consisted of a first coat of a black plastic compound, followed by a white protector coat. Jutting from the side window of the cockpit is an air valve.

A Douglas AC-47D with the number "927" stenciled under the nose and on the side of the left oil-cooler housing is parked at an unidentified air base. The photo originally was printed in February 1969, so the image was taken in or before that month. Below the cockpit window is the "Spooky" artwork associated with AC-47Ds from C Flight, 3rd Special Operations Squadron.

On February 24, 1969, during a night mission, this AC-47D, serial number 43-49770, from the 3rd Special Operations Squadron, was hit by an enemy mortar shell, blowing a 2-foot-wide hole through the right wing and riddling the fuselage with fragments. All the occupants of the main cabin, including Airman 1st Class John L. Levitow, the loadmaster, were wounded. Although stunned by the concussion of the blast and suffering from over forty fragment wounds in the back and legs, Levitow picked up an activated flare and managed to hurl it through the cargo door, saving the plane and the crew from destruction. For his conspicuous bravery, he was awarded the Congressional Medal of Honor. This photo shows the damage to the wing from the explosion of the mortar shell. Small holes from the mortar fragments are faintly visible on the fuselage.

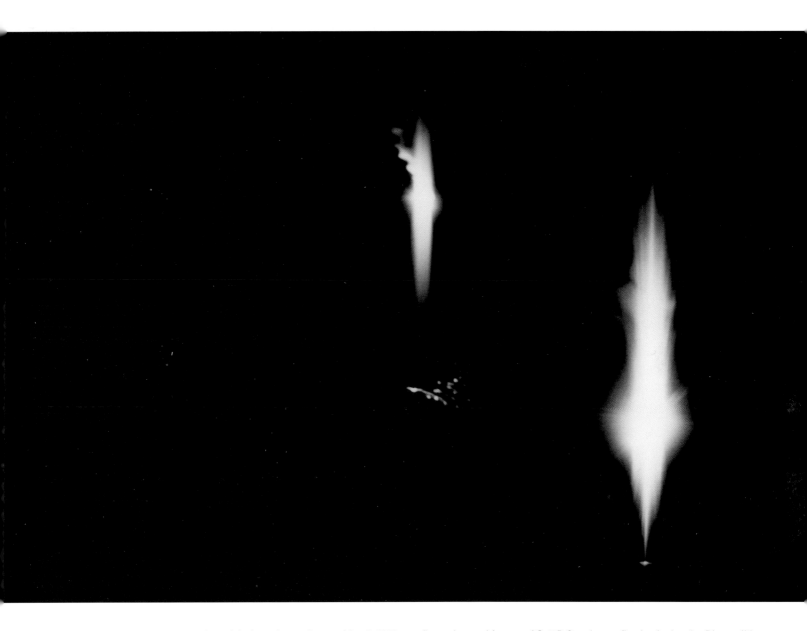

In a nighttime photo taken on May 6, 1969, two flares dropped from an AC-47D Spooky are flaming in the sky. Discernible below the flare to the left is Minigun fire from the Spooky.

Tracers from the Miniguns of an AC-47D, as well as illumination from four flares, visible not far above the horizon, light up the night sky in this time-exposure photograph.

In an ongoing effort to persuade Vietcong and North Vietnamese army troops to defect, Douglas C-47B-30-DK, serial number 44-76558, from the 9th Special Operations Squadron (Psychological Operations), 14th Special Operations Wing, is dropping leaflets over an enemy-held area in September 1969. The leaflets are issuing from a chute on the bottom of the fuselage, in line with the aft cargo door.

Two aircraft mechanics from the 6254th Air Base Group, Pleiku Air Base, Republic of Vietnam, Airman 1st Class William G. Simpson, *left*, and Airman 1st Class James H. Chester, are making connections on a newly mounted engine on a C-47 during April 1970.

Airmen Simpson and Chester are joined by TSgt. William G. Kearnes, in the white T-shirt, as the installation of a replacement engine proceeds. On the dome-shaped reduction-gear housing on the front of the engine is a sticker indicating that the engine had been overhauled by Gary Aircraft Corp.

By 1970, the US Air Force was phasing out the AC-47D Spooky gunships and transferred some of them to allied nations in Southeast Asia. The yellow, red, white, and blue national insignia of the Republic of Vietnam Air Force has been placed on the fuselage aft of the cargo door of this Spooky. Three Miniguns are protruding from the first three windows to the front of the cargo door.

Douglas C-47A-60-DL, serial number 43-30697, is parked at Phù Cát Air Base, Republic of Vietnam, on December 1, 1970. A logo for Orbit Airlines is to the rear of the cockpit; its significance is not clear. At some point in the Vietnam War, this aircraft was assigned as a transport to the 12th Tactical Fighter Wing, which was based at Phù Cát Air Base.

The same C-47A, with the Orbit Airlines logo, is viewed close-up at Phù Cát Air Base in December 1970. The cowlings of both engines have been removed, evidently for engine maintenance.

C-47B-30-DK, serial number 44-76558, from the 415th Transport Squadron, Republic of Vietnam Air Force, is parked on steel matting at Tan Son Nhut Air Base, Republic of Vietnam, in December 1970. The tail number is 4476558; above it is a circle with a small "E" and a large "V" on it.

The aft fuselage and empennage of the same C-47B are viewed close-up. On the rear cargo door is a square opening for a loudspeaker, for when the airplane was used in psychological operations.

Another Skytrain that flew with the Republic of Vietnam Air Force was Douglas C-47B-1-DK, serial number 43-48491 and tail number 4348491, parked on a flight line on December 15, 1970. In the circle on the tail is the code "EY."

C-47B-5-DK, serial number 43-48816, was converted to a C-47D at some point before it was transferred to the Republic of Vietnam Air Force, where it served with the 415th Transport Squadron. It was photographed at Tan Son Nhut Air Base on December 16, 1970. In the circle on the vertical fin are a small letter "E" and a large "S." Below the cockpit window is the crest of the 33rd Tactical Wing, the parent unit of the 415th Transport Squadron.

In a finish that appears to be white over aluminum paint, with a decorative stripe along the fuselage, this C-47, tail number 478686, assigned to the 314th Special Air Mission Squadron, Republic of Vietnam air force, is parked at Tan Son Nhut Air Base on December 15, 1970. Two men are scrubbing the aircraft, while another, *to the right*, hoses himself off.

A C-47, tail number 44457 (evidently, C-47B-25-DK, serial number 44-76457), painted in fresh Southeast Asia camouflage, is on display at Andrews Air Force Base, Maryland, in August 1972. The occasion was the celebration of the twenty-fifth anniversary of the founding of the US Air Force as a branch of the service separate from the US Army. *National Archives*